The Church and the Lord's Supper

CHARLES HODGE

"I am thrilled to see these articles from Charles Hodge put together in book form and made accessible for a wider audience. With clear writing, careful scholarship, and lucid argumentation, Hodge addresses some of the most important issues of ecclesiology in his day—which happen to still be some of the most important issues in our day. I hope that this volume will be read by many students, pastors, elders, and thoughtful Christians in our churches."

Kevin DeYoung
Senior Pastor, Christ Covenant Church (Matthews, NC);
Associate Professor of Systematic Theology,
Reformed Theological Seminary (Charlotte)

"Charles Hodge's concerns over the Oxford Movement in the Anglican Church and the Mercersburg Theology in the German Reformed Church remain as pertinent today as they were then. This is why Gary Steward's reprisal of these important controversies is so needed and timely. Will the significance of the church in its essentially invisible character prevail, or will some overly objective definition dominate? Some views circulating in Reformed circles today tend to undermine the Westminster Confession's definition of the church as 'the communion of saints,' thus rendering the church into a merely external organization. These views will result in nominalism and the politicization of the church's mission. We need to hear Hodge's warnings about the true character of the church, lest we end up subverting the gospel and the spiritual mission of the church to gather and perfect the saints."

Alan Strange
Professor of Church History,
Mid-America Reformed Seminary

The Church and the Lord's Supper

CHARLES HODGE

Edited by Gary Steward

The Church and the Lord's Supper

Copyright © 2024 Gary Steward
All rights reserved.

This book may not be reproduced, in whole or in part, without written permission from the publishers.

Joshua Press, West Lorne, Ontario (an imprint of H&E Publishing)
www.joshuapress.com

Paperback ISBN: 978-1-77484-150-1
eBook ISBN: 978-1-77484-151-8

Contents

Introduction	1
Chapter 1 A Summary of the Evangelical Doctrine of the Church	3
Chapter 2 Theories of the Church: A Critique of High Church Ritualism	7
Chapter 3 The Spiritual Nature of the Church	35
Chapter 4 The Visibility of the Church	85
Chapter 5 The Perpetuity of the Church	105
Chapter 6 The Reformed Protestant Doctrine of the Lord's Supper	137
Scripture Index	181

Introduction
by Gary Steward

The doctrines of the Church, the sacraments, and the gospel are all intertwined. The position one adopts in any one area necessarily affects the others. Certain views of the Lord's Supper can determine how one answers the fundamental question, "What must I do to be saved?" An evangelical answer to this question requires an evangelical view of the church and the sacraments.

Charles Hodge (1797–1878) was one of America's greatest nineteenth-century theologians. He understood the interrelated nature of these various doctrines. In his own day, Hodge believed that various views of the Church making inroads among Protestant evangelicals were undercutting the fundamental assertions of the Protestant gospel. Some of these views were being circulated in England by members of the High Church party of the Church of England, also known as "Tractarians" or adherents of "the Oxford Movement." In America, John Williamson Nevin and Phillip Schaff of Mercersburg, Pennsylvania, started a school of thought that promoted views of the church worked out against the backdrop of Second Great Awakening revivalism. Both of these groups elevated the institutional church and the administration of the sacraments to a degree that Hodge found alarming. Indeed, he believed these moves were nothing less than a reversion to Roman Catholicism and an abandonment of the evangelical gospel as traditionally espoused by Protestants.

It is against this backdrop that Hodge articulated his doctrine of the church in a number of articles that originally appeared in *The Princeton Review*. Hodge's main point in these articles was to

The Church and the Lord's Supper

assert that the Church of Jesus Christ is composed of all true believers who are spiritually united to Christ and to each other by the Holy Spirit. There is no external institution or organization that can lay claim to being the one true Church.

After reading the selected articles in this book, some may question whether Hodge's view necessarily leads to a Baptistic view of regenerate church membership. This was not the case for Hodge, and he did not follow any such implication in that direction. Hodge maintained the confessional Presbyterian views that the "visible church" consists of believers and their children, while the Church in its invisible and essentially spiritual nature consists only of Spirit-regenerated believers.[1]

Many in our own day are hungry for a mystical sense of the transcendent in their church experiences. Believers, having grown tired of faddish, therapeutic, consumeristic, and entertainment-oriented approaches to church life, are desirous of richer and more historical experiences. Many are thereby attracted to the kind of High Church ritualism and sacramentalism that Hodge felt was so destructive to personal faith in the gospel. He wrote these articles with a clear pastoral concern in mind, and it is with this same spirit and same concern that these articles are commended to you today.

The articles reprinted here have been slightly edited from how they first appeared in the volumes of *The Princeton Review*. All Latin and Greek has been translated, and minor changes have been made in capitalization, punctuation, and spelling to make these articles conform more closely with modern usage.

---

[1] Hodge's fullest argument for this view can be found in his article "The Church Membership of Infants," *Biblical Repertory and Princeton Review* 30 (1858): 347–389. See also Charles Hodge, "Bishop McIlvaine on the Church," *The Biblical Repertory and Princeton Review* 27 (1855): 355–357.

Chapter 1
A Summary of the Evangelical Doctrine of the Church[1]

The Church consists of those who are united to Christ by faith. He is the head; they severally are his members, collectively his body, which is the Church. As nothing but graduation is required to make a man an alumnus of a college, as all graduates are alumni, no one not a graduate is an alumnus; so nothing but faith in Christ is necessary to make a man a member of the true Church; all believers are members; and no one not a believer is or can be a member. The Church, therefore, consists of true believers scattered abroad throughout the world, united to Christ and to each other by the indwelling of the Holy Ghost.

Christ has commanded his people to associate themselves together in outward visible societies for the purposes of public worship, edification and mutual watch and care.

He has commanded them to receive into these societies, and to regard and treat as members of his body, all who, possessing competent knowledge, make a credible profession of faith and obedience. But as they cannot discern the heart, it must follow that many who are not true believers would be received into these societies, and be regarded and treated as members of the Church, before men, though they are not such in the sight of God. As union with the Church depends solely on union with Christ its head, by

---

[1] This chapter is excerpted from an article by Hodge entitled "Bishop McIlvaine on the Church," *The Biblical Repertory and Princeton Review* 27 (1855): 350-359. In this article, Hodge commended the Episcopalian Bishop Charles P. McIlvaine's evangelical doctrine of the church, as it appeared in McIlvaine's *The Truth and Life* (New York: Robert Carter, 1855).

faith, and not on union with these external societies; and as union with these societies, though a duty, is not in all cases essential, of course there may be members of the Church who are not members of these societies as there are members of these societies who are not members of the Church.

The attributes, prerogatives, and promises pertaining to the Church belong to the body of believers, and not to the external organization as such; and to these external organizations, only so far as they are what they profess to be, viz., associations of believers.

As we cannot discern the heart, we are bound to regard and treat as believers all who make a credible profession of faith, and to regard and treat all associations of credible believers for church purposes, as true Churches.

It is universally agreed that Christ has commanded his people to associate in external organizations, and that thus, as well as in other ways, the true Church becomes visible among men. But there is great diversity of opinion as to how far the mode of external organization is prescribed in the Scriptures. Some hold that nothing is absolutely enjoined on this subject, but that the Church is at liberty to assume what outward government she deems best suited to her circumstances. She may be Congregational, Presbyterian, or Prelatical, just as she sees fit, according to the saying of Stillingfleet, "Government is of God, the form of man;" and according to the analogy of civil governments, which may rightfully assume the democratical, aristocratical, or monarchical form, as the people may determine.[2] Secondly, others hold that while

---

[2] Edward Stillingfleet (1635–1699) was an Anglican clergyman and scholar. According to him, "[church government] is necessary by way of divine command...but which particular way or form it must be, is wholly left to the prudence of those in whose power and trust it is to see the peace of the church be secured on lasting foundations" (Edward Stillingfleete, *Irenicum: A Weapon-Salve for the Churches Wounds, or The Divine Right of Particular Forms of Church-Government: Discuss'd and Examin'd according to the Principles of the Law of Nature* (London: Henry Mortlock, 1662), 3.

A Summary

Christ has prescribed certain principles relating to the organization of the Church, he has left much, as to the details, discretionary. This is the common opinion of Protestants, and especially of Presbyterians; and whether recognized *in thesi*[3] or not, is practically acted upon by every religious denomination on earth. Thirdly, others again hold that everything in the government or polity of the Church is prescribed in the Scriptures; that the Church has no more discretion in this matter than she has in matters of doctrine; and that whatever is not enjoined, and, therefore, obligatory *jure divino*,[4] is forbidden and unlawful.

Any of these theories of Church government is consistent with the Protestant doctrine as to the nature of the Church. We may believe that the Church consists of true Christians, and yet believe that they are at liberty to assume what outward organization they please; or that their discretion is limited to matters of detail; or that they have no discretion in the premises. All that that doctrine requires, is that we hold that the Church is independent of all forms of external organization. She may exist under any form, or in the persons of scattered believers, for the obvious reason that she owes her existence not to outward organization, but to union with Christ. So long, therefore, as there are believers in the world, the Church is in the world. These believers are bound, whenever practicable, to unite in an outward organization; and the mode or form of that organization is, according to our doctrine, prescribed, to a certain extent, in the word of God; but the Church is no more dependent on such organization than the soul is upon the body.

---

[3] Latin for "as a proposition."
[4] Latin for "by divine right."

Chapter 2
Theories of the Church: A Critique of High Church Ritualism[1]

Archdeacon Manning and the Oxford School

This is one of the ablest productions of the Oxford school.[2] The theory of the church which that school has embraced, is here presented historically, in the first instance, and then sustained by arguments drawn from the design of the church, as a divine institute, and the common conclusion is arrived at and urged, that the one church, as described by the author, is the only revealed way of salvation. Archdeacon Manning's work has excited no little attention in England; and its republication in this country, has been warmly welcomed by the Oxford party in America.

We do not propose to make the book before us, the subject of particular examination; but simply to exhibit the theory of the church which it advocates, in connection and contrast with that which necessarily arises out of the evangelical system of doctrine. The church as an outward organization is the result and expression of an inward spiritual life; and consequently must take its form from the nature of the life whence it springs. This is only saying, in other words, that our theory of the church, depends on our theory of doctrine. If we hold a particular system of doctrine, we must

---

[1] This chapter was originally published by Hodge as "Theories of the Church," *The Biblical Repertory and Princeton Review* 18 (1846): 137-158. Hodge's essay was also reprinted in *The British and Foreign Evangelical Review* 1 (1852): 152-170.

[2] Hodge presented his essay on "the theories of the church" as a response to Henry Edward Manning's, *The Unity of the Church* (New York: D. Appleton & Co., 1844). Manning had asserted what Hodge refers to as a "Ritualistic" view of the church in this article. Manning, at the time, was a clergyman in the Church of England. He later converted to Roman Catholicism and became a Catholic priest in 1851.

7

hold a corresponding theory of the church. The two are so intimately connected that they cannot be separated; and it is doubtful whether, as a matter of experience, the system of doctrine most frequently leads to the adoption of a particular view of the church, or whether the view men take of the church more generally determines their system of doctrines. In the order of nature, and perhaps also most frequently in experience, the doctrine precedes the theory.

Three Forms of Christianity
History teaches us that Christianity appears under three characteristic forms; which for the sake of distinction may be called the Evangelical, the Ritual, and the Rationalistic. These forms always co-exist in the church, and are constantly striving for the mastery. At one period, the one, and at another, another gains the ascendency, and gives character to that period. During the apostolic age, the evangelical system prevailed, though in constant conflict with Ritualism in the form of Judaism. During the next age of the church we find Rationalism struggling for the ascendency, under the form of Gnosticism and the philosophy of the Platonizing fathers.

Ritualism, however, soon gained the mastery, which it maintained almost without a struggle until the time of the Reformation. At that period evangelical truth gained the ascendency which it maintained for more than a hundred years, and was succeeded on the continent by Rationalism, and in England, under Archbishop Laud, by Ritualism. This latter system, however, was there pressed beyond endurance, and the measures adopted for promoting it, led to a violent reaction. The restoration of Charles the II commenced the reign of the Rationalistic form of doctrine in England, manifesting itself in low Arminian or Pelagian views, and in general indifference. This continued to characterize the church in Great Britain, until the appearance of Wesley and Whitefield,

Theories of the Church

about a century ago, since which time there has been a constant advance in the prevalence and power of evangelical truth both in England and Scotland. Within the last ten or fifteen years, however, a new movement has taken place, which has attracted the attention of the whole Christian world.

After the fall of Archbishop Laud, the banishment of James II and the gradual disappearance of the non-jurors,[3] the principles which they represented, though they found here and there an advocate in the Church of England, lay nearly dormant, until the publication of the Oxford Tracts.[4] Since that time their progress has been rapid, and connected with the contemporaneous revival of Popery, constitutes the characteristic ecclesiastical features of the present generation. The church universal is so united, that no great movement in one portion of it, can be destitute of interest for all the rest. The church in this country, especially, is so connected with the church in Great Britain, there are so many channels of reciprocal influence between the two, that nothing of importance can happen there, which is not felt here. The church in the one country has generally risen and declined, with the church in the other. The spiritual death which gradually overspread England and Scotland from the revolution of 1688 to the rise of Wesley, in no small measure spread its influence over America; and the great revival of religion in England and Scotland before the middle

---

[3] William Laud (1573-1645), the Archbishop of Canterbury, advocated views associated with "High Church" ritualism, as opposed to the Puritans, who abhorred "formalism" and rituals not found in Scripture. King James II (r. 1685-1688) openly adhered to Roman Catholic doctrine and ritualism, and was deposed in the Glorious Revolution of 1688. Non-jurors refused to swear an oath of allegiance to William and Mary, his successors to the throne, but remained loyal to him and his successors. For this, they were referred to as "Jacobites," a title derived from *Jacobus*, the Latin form of James.

[4] *The Tracts for the Times* were published from 1833 to 1841 by leaders of the Oxford Movement, including John Henry Newman, John Keble, and Edward Bouverie Pusey. These writings launched the Oxford Movement, and adherence to their views became known as Tractarians.

of the last century, was contemporaneous with the revival which extended in this country from Maine to Georgia. The recent progress of Ritualism in England, is accompanied by the spread of the same principles in America. We are not, therefore, uninterested spectators of the struggle now in progress between the two conflicting systems of doctrines and theories of the church, the Evangelical and the Ritual. The spiritual welfare of our children and of the country is deeply concerned in the issue.

The different forms of religion to which reference has been made, have each its peculiar basis, both objective and subjective. The evangelical form rests on the scriptures as its objective ground; and its inward or subjective ground is an enlightened conviction of sin. The ritual system rests outwardly on the authority of the church, or tradition; inwardly on a vague religious sentiment. The rationalistic rests on the human understanding, and internally on indifference. These are general remarks, and true only in the general. Perhaps few persons are under the influence of any one of these forms, to the exclusion of the others; in very few, is the ground of belief exclusively the Bible, tradition, or reason. Yet as general remarks they appear to us correct, and may serve to characterize the comprehensive forms which the Christian religion has been found to assume.

The Evangelical View of the Church

The evangelical system of doctrine starts with the assumption that all men are under the condemnation and power of sin. This is assumed by the sacred writers as a fact of consciousness, and is made the ground of the whole doctrine of redemption. From the guilt of sin there is no method of deliverance but through the righteousness of Christ, and no way in which freedom from its power can be obtained, but through the indwelling of his Spirit. No man who is not united to Christ by a living faith is a partaker either of his righteousness or Spirit, and every man who does truly believe, is a partaker of both, so as to be both justified and sanctified. This union with Christ by the indwelling of his Spirit is always manifested by the fruits of righteousness; by love, joy, peace, longsuffering, gentleness, goodness, faith, meekness, temperance. Where these fruits of the Spirit are, there, and not elsewhere, is the Spirit; and where the Spirit is, there is union with Christ; and where union with Christ is, there is membership in his body, which is the Church. True believers, therefore, according to the scriptures, are the *kletoi*, the *eklektoi*, the *ekklesia*.[5] This is the fundamental principle of the evangelical theory respecting the church. It is the only view at all consistent with the evangelical system of doctrine; and as a historical fact, it is the view to which those doctrines have uniformly led. If a man holds that the church is the body of Christ; that the body of Christ consists of those in whom he dwells by his Spirit; that it is by faith we receive the promise of the Spirit; and that the presence of the Spirit is always manifested by his fruits; then he must hold that no man who does not possess that faith which works by love, is united to Christ or a member of his church; and that all, no matter how else they may differ, or where they may dwell, who have that faith, are members of that body, which is his church. Such is the unavoidable conclusion to which the evangelical system leads as to the nature of the church. The body to whom the attributes, the promises, the prerogatives of the church belong, consists of all true believers. This also is the turning point between the evangelical and ritual theories, on which all other questions concerning the church depend. To the question "What is the church?" or "Who constitute the church?" the Evangelicals answer, and must answer, "True believers." The answer of the Ritualists is "The organized professors of the true religion subject to lawful pastors." And according as the one or the other of these answers

---

[5] Greek for "the called," "the elect," and "the church."

is adopted, the one or the theory with its consequences of necessity follows.

The Visible and Invisible Church

The church, in that sense in which it is the heir of the promises and prerogatives granted in the word of God, consists of true believers, is in one aspect a visible, in another, an invisible body. First, believers as men are visible beings, and by their confession and fruits are visible as believers. "By their fruits ye shall know them."[6] In their character also of believers, they associate for the purposes of worship and discipline, and have their proper officers for instruction and government, and thus appear before the world as a visible body. And secondly, as God has not given to men the power to search the heart, the terms of admission into this body, or in other words, the terms of Christian communion, are not any infallible evidence of regeneration and true faith, but a credible profession. And as many make that profession who are either self-deceived or deceivers, it necessarily follows that many are of the church, who are not in the church. Hence arises the distinction between the real and the nominal, or, as it is commonly expressed, the invisible and the visible church. A distinction which is unavoidable, and which is made in all analogous cases, and which is substantially and of necessity admitted in this case even by those whose whole theory rests on the denial of it. The Bible promises great blessings to

Christians; but there are real Christians and nominal Christians; and no one hesitates to make the distinction and to confine the application of these promises to those who are Christians at heart, and not merely in name. The scriptures promise eternal life to believers. But there is a dead, as well as a living faith; there are true believers, and those who profess faith without possessing it.

---

[6] Matthew 7:20.

Theories of the Church

No one here again refuses to acknowledge the propriety of the distinction, or hesitates to say that the promise of eternal life belongs only to those who truly believe. In like manner there is a real and a nominal, a visible and an invisible church, a body consisting of those who are truly united to Christ, and a body consisting of all who profess such union. Why should not this distinction be allowed? How can what is said in scripture of the church, be applied to the body of professors, any more than what is said of believers, can be applied to the body of professed believers? There is the same necessity for the distinction in the one case, as in the other. And accordingly it is fact made by those who in terms deny it. Thus Mr. Palmer, an Oxford writer, says that the church, as composed of its vital and essential members, means "the elect and sanctified children of God" and adds that "it is generally allowed that the wicked belong only externally to the church."[7] Even Romanists are forced to make the same admission, when they distinguish between the living and dead members of the church. As neither they nor Mr. Palmer will contend that the promises pertain to the "dead" members, or those who are only externally united to the church, but must admit them to belong to the "essential" or "living" members, they concede the fundamental principle of the evangelical theory as to the nature of the church, viz., that it consists of true believers, and is visible as they are visible as believers by their profession and fruits, and that those associated with them in external union, are the church only outwardly, and not as constituent members of the body of Christ and temple of God. In this concession is involved an admission of the distinction for which the evangelical contend between the church invisible and visible,

---

[7] William Palmer, *A Treatise on the Church of Christ*, 2 vols. (London: J. G. & F. Rivington, 1838), 1:4. Palmer, a fellow of Magdalen College, Oxford, supported the Oxford Movement temporarily and converted to Roman Catholicism in 1855.

between nominal and real Christians, between true and professing believers.

The Unity of the Church

Such being the view of the nature of the church and of its visibility, to which the evangelical system of doctrine necessarily leads, it is easy to see wherein the church is one. If the church consists of those who are united to Christ and are the members of his body, it is evident that the bond which unites them to him, unites them to each other. They are one body in Christ Jesus, and every one members of one another. The vital bond between Christ and his body is the Holy Spirit, which he gives to dwell in all who are united to him by faith. The indwelling of the Spirit is therefore the essential or vital bond of unity in the church. By one Spirit we are all baptized into one body, for we are partakers of that one Spirit. The human body is one, because animated by one soul; and the church is one because actuated by one Spirit.

As the Spirit wherever he dwells manifests himself as the Spirit of truth, of love, and of holiness, it follows that those in whom he dwells must be one in faith, in love, and holy obedience. Those whom he guides, he guides into the knowledge of the truth, and as he cannot contradict himself, those under his guidance, must in all essential matters, believe the same truths. And as the Spirit of love, he leads all under his influence to love the same objects, the same God and Father of all, the same Lord Jesus Christ; and to love each other as brethren. This inward, spiritual union must express itself outwardly, in the profession of the same faith, in the cheerful recognition of all Christians as Christians, that is, in the communion of saints, and in mutual subjection. Every individual Christian recognizes the right of his fellow Christians to exercise over him a watch and care, and feels his obligation to submit to them in the Lord.

Theories of the Church

The Church's Organizational Divisions

Since however the church is too widely diffused for the whole to exercise their watch and care over each particular part, there is a necessity for more restricted organizations. Believers therefore of the same neighborhood, of the same province, of the same nation, may and must unite by some closer bond than that which externally binds the Church as a whole together. The Church of England is one, in virtue of its subjection to a common head, and the adoption of common formularies of worship and discipline. This more intimate union of its several parts with each other, does not in any measure violate its unity with the Episcopal body in this country. And the Presbyterian Church in the United States, though subject to its own peculiar judicatories, is still one with the Church of Scotland. It is evident, and generally conceded, that there is nothing, in independent organization, in itself considered, inconsistent with unity, so long as a common faith is professed, and mutual recognition is preserved. And if independent organization on account of difference of locality or of civil relations, is compatible with unity, so also is independent organization on the ground of diversity of language. The former has its foundation in expediency and convenience, so has the latter. It is not true, therefore, as Ritualists teach, that there cannot be two independent churches, in the same place. Englishmen in Germany and Germans in England may organize churches not in organic connection with those around them, with as much propriety as Episcopalians in England and Episcopalians in Scotland may have independent organizations.

Still further, as independent or separate organization is admitted to be consistent with true unity, by all but Romanists, it follows that any reason not destructive of the principle of unity, may be made the ground of such separate organization; not merely difference as to location, or diversity of language, but diversity of opinion. It is on all hands conceded that there may be difference of opinion, within certain limits, without violating unity of faith; and it is also admitted that there may be independent organization, for considerations of convenience, without violating the unity of communion. It therefore follows, that where such diversity of opinion exists, as to render such separate organization convenient, the unity of the church is not violated by such separation. Diversity of opinion is indeed an evidence of imperfection, and therefore such separations are evil, so far as they are evidence of want of perfect union in faith. But they are a less evil, than, either hypocrisy or contention; and therefore, the diversity of sects, which exist in the Christian world, is to be regarded as incident to imperfect knowledge and imperfect sanctification. They are to be deplored, as every other evidence of such imperfection is to be regretted, yet the evil is not to be magnified above its just dimensions. So long as unity of faith, of love, and of obedience is preserved, the unity of the church is as to its essential principle safe. It need hardly be remarked, that it is admitted that all separate organization on inadequate grounds, and all diversity of opinion affecting important doctrines, and all want of Christian love and especially a sectarian, unchurching spirit, are opposed to the unity of the church, and either mar or destroy it according to their nature.

The sense in which the church is catholic depends on the sense in which it is one. It is catholic only as it is one. If its unity, therefore, depends on subjection to one visible head, to one supreme governing tribunal, to the adoption of the same form of organization, then of course its extent or catholicity are limited by these conditions. If such be the nature of its oneness, then all not subject to such visible head, or governing tribunal, or who do not adopt the form of government assumed to be necessary, are excluded from the church. But if the unity of the church arises from union with Christ and the indwelling of his Spirit, then all who are thus united to him, are members of his church, no matter what their

Theories of the Church

external ecclesiastical connections may be, or whether they sustain any such relations at all. And as all really united to Christ are the true church, so all who profess such union by professing to receive his doctrines and obey his laws, constitute the professing or visible church. It is plain therefore that the evangelical are the most truly catholic, because, embracing in their definition of the church all who profess the true religion, they include a far wider range in the church catholic, than those who confine their fellowship to those who adopt the same form of government, or are subject to the same visible head.

The Essential Mark of a True Church

It is easy to see how, according to the evangelical system, the question, "What is a true church" is to be answered. Starting with the principle that all men are sinners, that the only method of salvation is by faith in Jesus Christ, and that all who believe in Him, and show the fruits of faith in a holy life, are the children of God, the called according to his purpose--that is, in the language of the New Testament, the *kletoi*, the *ekklesia*,[8] that system must teach that all true believers are members of the true church, and all professors of the true faith are members of the visible church. This is the only conclusion to which that system can lead. And therefore the only essential mark of a true church which it can admit, is the profession of the true religion. Any individual man who makes a credible profession of religion we are bound to regard as a Christian; any society of such men, united for the purpose of worship and discipline, we are bound to regard as a church. As there is endless diversity as to the degree of exactness with which individual Christians conform, in their doctrines, spirit and deportment, to the word of God, so there is great diversity as to the degree in which the different churches conform to the same standard. But as in the

---

[8] Greek for "called" and "church."

case of the individual professor we can reject none who does not reject Christ, so in regard to churches, we can disown none who holds the fundamental doctrines of the gospel.

Objections to the Evangelical Understanding of the Church Answered

Against this simple and decisive test of a true church it is objected on the one hand, that it is too latitudinarian. The force of this objection depends upon the standard of liberality adopted. It is of course too latitudinarian for Romanists and High churchmen, as well as for rigid sectarians. But is it more liberal than the Bible, and our own Confession of Faith? Let any man decide this question by ascertaining what the Bible teaches as the true answer to the question, what is a Christian? And what is a church? You cannot possibly make your notion of a church narrower than your notion of a Christian. If a true Christian is a true believer, and a professed believer is a professing Christian, then of course a true church is a body of true Christians, a professing or visible church is a body of professing Christians. This is the precise doctrine of our standards, which teach that the church consists of all those who profess the true religion.[9]

On the other hand, however, it is objected that it cannot be expected of ordinary Christians that they should decide between the conflicting creeds of rival churches, and therefore the profession of the truth cannot be the mark of a true church. To this objection it may be answered first, that it is only the plain fundamental doctrines of the gospel which are necessary to salvation, and therefore it is the profession of those doctrines alone, which is necessary to

---

[9] According to the Westminster Confession of Faith, "The visible church...consists of all those, throughout the world, that profess the true religion, and of their children" (XXV.ii). While Hodge does not include the children of professing believers here, this is the view he argues for elsewhere. See Charles Hodge, "The Church Membership of Infants," *Biblical Repertory and Princeton Review* 30 (1858): 347–389.

Theories of the Church

establish the claim of any society to be regarded as a portion of the true church. Secondly, that the objection proceeds on the assumption that such doctrines cannot by the people be gathered from the word of God. If however the scriptures are the rule of faith, so plain that all men may learn from them what they must believe and do in order to be saved, then do they furnish an available standard by which they may judge of the faith both of individuals and of churches. Fourthly, this right to judge and the promise of divine guidance in judging are given in the scriptures to all the people of God, and the duty to exercise the right is enjoined upon them as a condition of salvation. They are pronounced accursed if they do not try the spirits, or if they receive any other gospel than that taught in the scriptures.[10] And fifthly, this doctrinal test is beyond comparison more easy of application than any other. How are the unlearned to know that the church with which they are connected has been derived, without schism or excommunication, from the churches founded by the apostles? What can they tell of the apostolical succession of pastors? These are mere historical questions, the decision of which requires great learning, and involves no test of character, and yet the salvation of men is made to depend on that decision. All the marks of the church laid down by Romanists and High-churchmen, are liable to two fatal objections. They can be verified, if at all, only by the learned. And secondly, when verified, they decide nothing. A church may have been originally founded by the apostles, and possess an uninterrupted succession of pastors, and yet be now a synagogue of Satan.[11]

The theory of the church, then, which of necessity follows from the evangelical system of doctrine is, that all who really believe the gospel constitute the true church, and all who profess such faith constitute the visible church; that in virtue of the profession of his

---

[10] See 1 John 4:1 and Galatians 1:8.
[11] See Revelation 2:9, 3:9. See also the Westminster Confession of Faith (XXV.v).

common faith, and of allegiance to the same Lord, they are one body, and in this one body there may rightly be subordinate and more intimate unions of certain parts, for the purposes of combined action, and of mutual oversight and consolation. When it is said, in our Confession of Faith, that out of this visible church, "there is no ordinary possibility of salvation," it is only saying that there is no salvation without the knowledge and profession of the gospel; that there is no other name by which we must be saved, but the name of Jesus Christ.[12] The proposition that "out of the church there is no salvation" is true or false, liberal or illiberal, according to the latitude given to the word "church." There was not long since, and probably there is still in New York a little society of Sandemanian Baptists, consisting of seven persons, two men and five women, who hold that they constitute the whole church in America.[13] In their mouths the proposition above stated would indeed be restrictive. In the mouth of a Romanist, it means there is no salvation to any who do not belong to that body which acknowledges the Pope as its head. In the mouths of High Churchmen, it means there is no salvation to those who are not in subjection to some prelate who is in communion with the church catholic. While in the mouths of Protestants, it means there is no salvation without faith in Jesus Christ.

The Ritualistic View of the Church, Priesthood, Sacraments, and Salvation

The system, which for the sake of distinction has been called the Ritual, agrees of course with the evangelical as to many points of doctrine. It includes the doctrine of the Trinity, of the incarnation

---

[12] Westminster Confession of Faith (XXV.ii).

[13] The Sandemanians were followers of John Glas (1695–1773) and Robert Sandeman (1718–1771) who held an intellectualistic view of saving faith, an antinomian view of the Christian life, and a rigid exclusivity regarding their own churches. Sandemanian churches ceased to exist in America before the end of the nineteenth century.

Theories of the Church

of the Son of God, of original sin, of the sacrifice of Christ as a satisfaction to satisfy divine justice, of the supernatural influence of the Holy Spirit in regeneration and sanctification, of the resurrection of the body and of an eternal judgment. The great distinction lies in the answer which it gives the question, "What must I do to be saved?" or "By what means does the soul become interested in the redemption of Christ?" According to the Evangelical system, it is faith. Every sinner who hears the gospel has unimpeded access to the Son of God, and can, in the exercise of faith and repentance, go immediately to him, and obtain eternal life at his hands.

According to the Ritual system, he must go to the priest; the sacraments are the channels of grace and salvation, and the sacraments can only be lawfully or effectively administered by men prelatically ordained.[14] The doctrine of the priestly character of the Christian ministry, therefore, is one of the distinguishing characteristics of the Ritual system. A priest is a man ordained for men, in things pertaining to God, to offer gifts and sacrifices. The very nature of the office supposes that those for whom he acts, have not in themselves liberty of access to God; and therefore the Ritual system is founded on the assumption that we have not this liberty of drawing nigh to God. It is only by the ministerial intervention of the Christian priesthood, that the sinner can be reconciled and made a partaker of salvation. Here then is a broad line of distinction between the two systems of doctrines. This was one of the three great doctrines rejected by Protestants, at the time of the Reformation. They affirmed the priesthood of all believers, asserting that all have access to God through the High Priest of their profession, Jesus, the Son of God; and they denied the official priesthood of the clergy.

---

[14] i.e., ordained by a bishop within the church hierarchy.

The Church and the Lord's Supper

The second great distinction between the two systems of doctrine, is the place they assign the sacraments. The evangelical admit them to be efficacious signs of grace, but they ascribe their efficacy not to any virtue in them or in him by whom they are administered, but to the influence of the Spirit in them that do by faith receive them. Ritualists attribute to them an inherent virtue, an *opus operatum* efficacy, independent of the moral state of the recipient.[15] According to the one system, the sacraments are necessary only as matters of precept; according to the other, they have the necessity of means. According to the one, we are required to receive baptism, just as we are under obligation to keep the Sabbath, or as the Jews were required to be circumcised, and yet we are taught that if any man kept the law, his uncircumcision should be counted for circumcision. And thus also, if any one truly repents and believes, his want of baptism cannot make the promise of God of none effect. The neglect of such instituted rites may involve more or less sin, or none at all, according to the circumstances. It is necessary only as obedience to any other positive institution is necessary; that is, as a matter of duty, the non-performance of which ignorance or disability may palliate or excuse. According to the latter system, however, we are required to receive baptism because it is the only appointed means of conveying to us the benefits of redemption. It is of the same necessity as faith. It is a *sine qua non*. This alters the whole nature of the case, and changes in a great measure the plan of redemption.

The theory of the church connected with the Ritual system of doctrine, that system which makes ministers priests, and the sacraments the only appointed channels of communicating to men the benefits of redemption, is implied in the nature of the doctrines themselves. It makes the church so prominent that Christ

---

[15] *Opus operatum* literally mean "the work wrought," as if the sacrament in and of itself communicates efficacious grace simply by being performed or "wrought."

Theories of the Church

and the truth are eclipsed. This made Dr. Parr call the whole system "Churchianity," in distinction from Christianity.[16]

If our Lord, when he ascended to heaven, clothed his apostles with all the power which he himself possessed in his human nature, so that they were to the church what he himself had been, its infallible teachers and the dispensers of pardon and grace; and if in accordance with that assumption, the apostles communicated this power to their successors, the prelates, then it follows that these prelates, and those whom they may authorize to act in their name, are the dispensers of truth and salvation, and communion with them, or subjection to their authority, is essential to union with the church and to eternal life. The church is thus represented as a storehouse of divine grace; whose treasures are in the custody of its officers, to be dealt out by them, and at their discretion. It is like one of the rich convents of the Middle Ages; to whose gates the people repaired at stated times for food. The convent was the storehouse. Those who wanted food must come to its gates. Food was given at the discretion of its officers, to what persons and on what conditions they saw fit. To obtain supplies, it was of course necessary to recognize the convent as the depository, and its officers as the distributors; and none who refuse such recognition, could be fed from its stores. The analogy fails indeed as to an essential point. Food could be obtained elsewhere than at the convent gates; and none need apply, who did not choose to submit to the prescribed conditions. Whereas according to Ritualists, the food of the soul can be obtained nowhere but at the doors of the church; and those who refuse to receive it there, and at the hands of authorized ministers, and on the terms they prescribe, cannot receive it at all. Unless in communion of the church we cannot be

---

[16] This is a reference to Samuel Parr (1747–1825), an Anglican clergyman and literary critic. See John Johnstone, ed., *The Works of Samuel Parr*, 8 vols. (London: Longman, Rees, et al., 1828), 1:341.

saved; and unless in subjection to prelates deriving the gift of the Spirit by regular succession from the apostles, we cannot be in communion of the church. The subjection to the bishop, therefore, is an indispensable condition of salvation. He is the center of unity; the bond of union between the believer and the church and thus with Christ.

The unity of the church, according to this theory, is no longer a spiritual union; not a unity of faith and love, but a union of association, a union of connection with the authorized dispensers of saving grace. It is not enough for any society of men to show that they are united in faith with the apostles, and in heart with all the people of God, and with Christ by the indwelling of his Spirit, as manifested by his fruits, they cannot be recognized as any portion of the true church, unless they can prove historically their descent as a society from the apostles through the line of bishops. They must prove themselves a church, just as a man proves his title to an estate. No church, says Mr. Palmer, not founded by the apostles, or regularly descended from such a church without separation or excommunication, can be considered a true church; and every society that can make out such a descent, is a true church, for a church can only cease to be united to Christ by its own act of separation, or by the lawful judgment of others.[17]

The Ritualists' Doctrine of "Apostolic Succession"

This also is what is meant by apostolicity as an attribute and mark of the church. A church is not apostolical because it holds the doctrines, and conforms to the institutions of the apostles, but because it is historically derived from them by an uninterrupted descent. "Any society which is in fact derived from the apostles, must be so by spiritual propagation, or derivation, or union, not by separation from the apostles or the churches actually derived from their

---

[17] Palmer, *Treatise on the Church of Christ*, 1:309-404.

Theories of the Church

preaching, under pretense of establishing a new system of supposed apostolic perfection. Derivation from the apostles, is, in the former case, a reality, just as much as the descent of an illustrious family from its original founder. In the latter case it is merely an assumption in which the most essential links of the genealogy are wanting."[18] This descent must be through prelates, who are the bonds of connection between the apostles and the different portions of the one catholic and apostolic church. Without regular consecration there can be no bishop; and without a bishop no church, and out of the church no salvation.

The application of these principles as made by their advocates, reveals their nature and importance, more distinctly than any mere verbal statement of them. The Methodists, for example, though they adopt the doctrinal standards of the Church of England, and have the same form of government, are not and never can become, according to this theory, a part of the church, because the line of descent was broken by Wesley. He was but a presbyter and could not continue the succession of the ministry. A fatal flaw thus exists in their ecclesiastical pedigree, and they are hopelessly cut off from the church and from salvation.[19]

The Roman and Eastern churches, on the contrary, are declared to be true churches, because descended from the communions founded by the apostles, and because they have never been separated from the church catholic either by voluntary secession or by excommunication. The Nestorians, on the other hand, are declared to be no part of the true church; for though they may now

---

[18] Palmer, *Treatise on the Church of Christ*, 1:160.
[19] John Wesley (1703-1791) never formally separated himself from the Church of England, but he ordained a number of men to be ministers in the newly emerging Methodist Church.

have the orthodox faith, and though they have preserved the succession of bishops, they were excommunicated in the fifth century, and that sentence has never been revoked.[20]

The Church of England is declared to be a true church, because it has preserved the succession, and because, although excommunicated by the Church of Rome, that sentence has not been ratified by the church universal. All other ecclesiastical societies in Great Britain and Ireland, whether Romanist or Protestant, are pronounced to be cut off from the church and out of the way of salvation. This position is openly avowed, and is the necessary consequence of the theory. As the Romanists in those countries, though they have the succession, yet they voluntarily separate themselves from the Church of England, which as that is a true church, is to separate themselves from the church of Christ, a sin which is declared to be of the same turpitude as adultery and murder, and as certainly excludes from heaven. As to all other Protestant bodies, the case is still plainer. They have not only separated from the church, but lost the succession, and are therefore out of the reach of the benefits of redemption, which flow only in the line of that succession.

The Church of Scotland is declared to be in the same deplorable condition. Though under the Stuarts episcopacy was established in that country, yet it was strenuously resisted by the people; and under William III it was, by a joint act of the Assembly and Parliament formally rejected; they thereby separated themselves from the successors of the apostles, "and all the temporal enactments and powers of the whole world could not cure this fault, nor

---

[20] Nestorians, so named after the Archbishop of Constantinople Nestorius (386-450), asserted that the divine and human natures of the incarnate Christ remain divided into two separate persons. Nestorianism was condemned as heretical at the Council of Ephesus (431) and the Council of Chalcedon (451). Chalcedon asserted that orthodox position that Christ possesses two distinct natures in one person.

Theories of the Church

render them a portion of the church of Christ."[21] The same judgment is pronounced on all the churches in this country except the Church of England. The Romanists here are excluded, because they are derived from the schismatic Papists in Great Britain and Ireland, or have intruded into sees where bishops deriving authority from the Anglican Church already presided. How this can be historically made out as regards Maryland, and Louisiana, it is not for us to say. The theory forbids the existence of two separate churches in the same place. If the Church of England in Maryland is a true church, the Church of Rome is not. Bishop Whittingham, therefore, with perfect consistency, always speaks of the Romanists in the United States as schismatics, and schismatics of course are out of the church.[22] As to non-episcopal communions in this country, they are not only declared to be in a state of schism, but to be destitute of the essential elements of the church. They are all, therefore, of necessity excluded from the pale of the church. The advocates of this theory, when pressed with the obvious objection that multitudes thus excluded from the church, and consequently from salvation, give every evidence of piety, meet the objection by quoting Augustine, "Let us hold it as a thing unshaken and firm, that no good men *can* divide themselves from the church."[23] "It is not indeed to be supposed or believed for a moment," adds Mr. Palmer, "that divine grace would permit the really holy and justified members of Christ to fall from the way of life. He would only permit the unsanctified, the enemies of Christ to sever themselves from that fountain, where his Spirit is freely given." Voluntary separation therefore from the church, he concludes is "a sin which, unless repented of, is eternally destructive of the soul. The heinous

---

[21] Palmer, *Treatise on the Church of Christ*, 1:576.
[22] William Whittingham was the Episcopal Bishop of Maryland from 1840–1879.
[23] Augustine made this remark in reference to the Donatists around the beginning of the fifth century.

nature of this offence is incapable of exaggeration, because no human imagination, and no human tongue can adequately describe its enormity."[24] The only church in Great Britain, according to Mr. Palmer, be it remembered, is the Church of England, and the only church in this country according to the same theory and its advocates, is the Episcopal Church. Thus the knot is fairly cut. It is apparently a formidable difficulty, that there should be more piety out of the church, than in it. But the difficulty vanishes at once, when we know that "no good man *can* divide himself from the church."

If this theory were new, if it were now presented for the first time, it would be rejected with indignation and derision; indignation at its monstrous and unscriptural claims, and derision at the weakness of the arguments by which it is supported. But age renders even imbecility venerable. It must also be conceded that a theory which has for centuries prevailed in the church, must have something to recommend it. It is not difficult to discover, in the present case, what that something is. The Ritual theory of the church is perfectly simple and consistent. It has the first and most important element of success in being intelligible. That Christ should found a church, or external society, giving to his apostles the Holy Spirit to render them infallible in teaching and judging, and authorize them to communicate the like gift to their successors to the end of time; and make it a condition of salvation that all should recognize their spiritual authority, receive their doctrines and submit to their decisions, declaring that what they bound on earth should be bound in heaven, and what they loosed on earth should be loosed in heaven, is precisely the plan which the wise men of this world would have devised. It is in fact that which they have constructed. We must not forget, however, that the wisdom of men is foolishness with God.

---

[24] Palmer, *Treatise on the Church of Christ*, 1:54.

Theories of the Church

Again, this theory admits of being propounded in the forms of truth. All its fundamental principles may be stated in a form to command universal assent. It is true that the church is one; that it is catholic and apostolical; that it has the power of authoritative teaching and judging; that out of its pale there is no salvation. But this system perverts all these principles. It places the bond of unity in the wrong place. Instead of saying with Jerome, "*Ecclesia ibi est, ubi vera fides est*,"[25] or with Irenaeus, "*ubi Spiritus Dei, illic ecclesia*,"[26] they assume that the church is nowhere, where prelates are not. The true apostolicity of the church, does not consist in an external descent to be historically traced from the early churches, but in sameness of faith and Spirit with the apostles. Separation from the church is indeed a great sin; but there is no separation from the church involved in withdrawing from an external body whose terms of communion hurt the enlightened conscience; provided this be done without excommunicating or denouncing those who are really the people of God.

The Allure and Danger of the Ritualistic System

The great advantage of this theory, however, is to be found in its adaptation to the human heart. Most men who live where the gospel is known, desire some better foundation for confidence towards God, than their own good works. To such men the church, according to this theory, presents itself as an Institute of Salvation; venerable for its antiquity, attractive from the number and rank of its disciples, and from the easy terms on which it proffers pardon and eternal life. There are three very comprehensive classes of men to whom this system must commend itself. The first consists of those who are at once ignorant and wicked. The degraded inhabitants of Italy and Portugal have no doubt of their salvation, no

---

[25] "There the church is, where there is truth faith."
[26] "Where the Spirit of God is, there is the church."

matter how wicked they may be, so long as they are in the church and submissive to officers and rites. The second includes those who are devout and at the same time ignorant of the scriptures. Such men feel the need of religion, of communion with God, and of preparation for heaven. But knowing nothing of the gospel, or disliking what they know, a form of religion which is laborious, mystical, and ritual, meets all their necessities, and commands their homage. The third class consists of worldly men, who wish to enjoy this life and get to heaven with as little trouble as possible. Such men, the world over, are high churchmen. To them a church which claims the secure and exclusive custody of the blessings of redemption, and which she professes to grant on the condition of unresisting submission to her authority and rites, is exactly the church they desire. We need not wonder, therefore, at the long continued and extensive prevalence of this system. It is too much in accordance with the human heart to fail of its support, or to be effectually resisted by any power short of that by which the heart is changed.

It is obvious that the question concerning the nature and prerogatives of the church, is not one which relates to the externals of religion. It concerns the very nature of Christianity and the conditions of salvation. If the soul convinced of sin and desirous of reconciliation with God, is allowed to hear the Savior's voice, and permitted to go to him by faith for pardon and the Spirit, then the way of life is unobstructed. But if a human priest must intervene, and bar our access to Christ, assuming the exclusive power to dispense the blessings Christ has purchased, and to grant or withhold them at discretion, then the whole plan of salvation is effectually changed. No sprinkling priest, no sacrificial or sacramental rite can be substituted for the immediate access of the soul to Christ, without imminent peril of salvation.

Harm Brought by the Ritualistic System to the Christian Life

Theories of the Church

It is not, however, merely the first approach to God, or the commencement of a religious life, that is perverted by the ritual system; all the inward and permanent exercises of religion must be modified and injured by it. It produces a different kind of religion from that which we find portrayed in the Bible, and exemplified in the lives of the apostles and early Christians. There, every thing is spiritual. God and Christ are the immediate objects of reverence and love; communion with the Father of Spirits through Jesus Christ his Son, and by the Holy Ghost, is the life which is there exhibited. In the Ritual system, rites, ceremonies, altars, buildings, priests, saints, the blessed virgin, intervene and divide or absorb the reverence and homage due to God alone. If external rites and creature agents are made necessary to our access to God, then those rites and agents will more or less take the place of God, and men will come to worship the creature rather than the creator. This tendency constantly gathers strength, until actual idolatry is the consequence, or until all religion is made to consist in the performance of external services. Hence this system is not only destructive of true religion, but leads to security in the indulgence of sin and commission of crimes. Though it includes among its advocates many devout and exemplary men, its legitimate fruits are recklessness and profligacy, combined with superstition and bigotry. It is impossible, also, under this system, to avoid transferring the subjection of the understanding and conscience due to God and his word, to the church and the priesthood. The judgments of the church, considered as an external visible society, are pronounced even by the Protestant advocates of this theory, to be unerring and irrefragable, to which every believer must bow on pain of perdition.[27] The bishops are declared to stand in Christ's place; to be clothed with all the authority which he as man possessed; to be invested with the power to communicate the Holy Ghost, to

---

[27] Palmer, *Treatise on the Church*, 2:46.

forgive sins, to make the body and blood of Christ, and to offer sacrifices available for the living and the dead. Such a system must exalt the priesthood into the place of God.

A theory, however, which has so long prevailed need not be judged by its apparent tendencies. Let it be judged by its fruits. It has always and everywhere, just in proportion to its prevalence, produced the effects above referred to. It has changed the plan of salvation; it has rendered obsolete the answer given by Paul to the question, "What must I do to be saved?" It has perverted religion. It has introduced idolatry. It has rendered men secure in the habitual commission of crime. It has subjected the faith, the conscience, and the conduct of the people to the dictation of the priesthood. It has exalted the hierarchy, saints, angels, and the Virgin Mary, into the place of God, so as to give a polytheistic character to the religion of a large part of Christendom. Such are the actual fruits of that system which has of late renewed its strength, and which everywhere asserts its claims to be received as genuine Christianity.

Conclusion

It will not be necessary to dwell on that theory of the church which is connected with Rationalism. Its characteristic feature is, that the church is not a divine institution, with prerogatives and attributes authoritatively determined by its author, but rather a form of Christian society, to be controlled according to the wisdom of its members. It may be identified with the state, or made dependent on it; or erected into a coordinate body with its peculiar officers and ends. It is obvious that a system which sets aside, more or less completely, the authority both of scripture and tradition, must leave its advocates at liberty to make of the church just what "the exigency of the times" in their judgment requires. The philosophical or mystic school of Rationalists, have of course a mystical doctrine of the church, which can be understood only by those who understand the philosophy on which it rests. With these views we have in this country little concern, nor do we believe they are destined to excite any general interest, or to exert any permanent influence. The two theories of the church which are now in obvious conflict, are the Evangelical and Ritual. The controversy between Protestants and Romanists, has, in appearance, shifted its ground from matters of doctrine to the question concerning the church. This is, however, only a change in form. The essential question remains the same. It is still a contention about the very nature of religion, and the method of salvation.

Chapter 3
The Spiritual Nature of the Church[1]

The Church as the Communion of Saints

In that symbol of faith adopted by the whole Christian world, commonly called the Apostles' Creed, the Church is declared to be "the communion of saints." In analyzing the idea of the Church here presented, it may be proper to state, first, what is not included in it; and secondly, what it does really embrace.

It is obvious that the Church, considered as the communion of saints, does not necessarily include the idea of a visible society organized under one definite form. A kingdom is a political society governed by a king; an aristocracy is such a society governed by a privileged class; a democracy is a political organization having the power centered in the people. The very terms suggest these ideas. There can be no kingdom without a king, and no aristocracy without a privileged class. There may, however, be a communion of saints without a visible head, without prelates, without a democratic covenant. In other words, the Church, as defined in the creed, is not a monarchy, an aristocracy, or a democracy. It may be either, all, or neither. It is not, however, presented as a visible organization, to which the form is essential, as in the case of the human societies just mentioned.

Again, the conception of the Church as the communion of saints, does not include the idea of any external organization. The bond of union may be spiritual. There may be communion without external organized union. The Church, therefore, according to

---

[1] This chapter was originally published by Hodge as "Idea of the Church," *The Biblical Repertory and Princeton Review* 25 (1853): 249–290.

this view, is not essentially a visible society; it is not a corporation which ceases to exist if the external bond of union be dissolved. It may be proper that such union should exist; it may be true that it has always existed; but it is not necessary. The Church, as such, is not a visible society. All visible union, all external organization, may cease, and yet, so long as there are saints who have communion, the Church exists, if the Church is the communion of saints. That communion may be in faith, in love, in obedience to a common Lord. It may have its origin in something deeper still; in the indwelling of the Holy Spirit, even the Spirit of Christ, by which every member is united to Christ, and all the members are joined in one body. This is a union far more real, a communion far more intimate, than subsists between the members of any visible society as such. So far, therefore, is the Apostles' Creed from representing the Church as a monarchy, an aristocracy, or a democracy; so far is it from setting forth the Church as a visible society of one specific form that it does not present it under the idea of an external society at all. The saints may exist, they may have communion, the Church may continue under any external organization, or without any visible organization whatever.

The Saints in the Church

What is affirmed in the above cited definition is, first, that the Church consists of saints; and, secondly, of saints in communion—that is, so united as to form one body. To determine, therefore, the true idea of the Church, it is only necessary to ascertain who are meant by the "saints," and the nature of their communion, or the essential bond by which they are united.

The word *hagios*, "saint," signifies holy, worthy of reverence, pure, in the sense of freedom either from guilt, or from moral pollution. The word *hagiazein* means to render holy or sacred, to cleanse from guilt, as by a sacrifice, or from moral defilement, by the renewing of the heart. The saints, therefore, according to the scriptural meaning of the term, are those who have been cleansed from guilt or justified, who have been inwardly renewed or sanctified, and who have been separated from the world and consecrated to God. Of such the Church consists. If a man is not justified, sanctified, and consecrated to God, he is not a saint, and therefore does not belong to the Church, which is the communion of saints.

Under the old dispensation, the whole nation of the Hebrews was called holy, as separated from the idolatrous nations around them, and consecrated to God. The Israelites were also called the children of God, as the recipients of his peculiar favors. These expressions had reference rather to external relations and privileges than to internal character. In the New Testament, however, they are applied only to the true people of God. None are there called saints but the sanctified in Christ Jesus. None are called the children of God, but those horn of the Spirit, who being children are heirs, heirs of God, and joint heirs with Jesus Christ of a heavenly inheritance. When, therefore, it is said that the Church consists of saints, the meaning is not that it consists of all who are externally consecrated to God, irrespective of their moral character, but that it consists of true Christians or sincere believers.

The Spiritual Unity of the Church

As to the bond by which the saints are united so as to become a church, it cannot be anything external, because that may and always does unite those who are not saints. The bond, whatever it is, must be peculiar to the saints; it must be something to which their justification, sanctification, and access to God are due. This can be nothing less than their relation to Christ. It is in virtue of union with him that men become saints, or are justified, sanctified, and brought nigh to God. They are one body in Christ Jesus. The bond of union between Christ and his people is the Holy Spirit, who dwells in him and in them. He is the head, they are the members of his body, the Church, which is one body, because pervaded and animated by one Spirit. The proximate and essential bond of union between the saints, that which gives rise to their communion, and makes them the Church or body of Christ, is, therefore, the indwelling of the Holy Ghost.

Such, then, is the true idea of the Church, or, what is the same thing, the idea of the true Church. It is the communion of saints, the body of those who are united to Christ by the indwelling of his Spirit. The two essential points included in this definition are, that the Church consists of saints, and that the bond of their union is not external organization, but the indwelling of the Holy Spirit. These, therefore, are the two points to be established. As, however, the one involves the other, they need not be considered separately. The same arguments which prove the one, prove also the other.

By this statement, it is not meant that the word church is not properly used in various senses. The object of inquiry is not the usage of a word, but the true idea of a thing; not how the word "church" is employed, but what the Church itself is. Who compose the Church? What is essential to the existence of that body, to which the attributes, the promises, the prerogatives of the Church belong? On the decision of that question rests the solution of all other questions in controversy between Romanists and Protestants.

Scriptural Arguments for Defining the Church
The holy Scriptures are on this, as on all other matters of faith or practice, our only infallible rule. We may confirm our interpretation of the Scriptures from various sources, especially from the current judgment of the Church, but the real foundation of our faith is to be sought in the word of God itself. The teachings of the Scriptures concerning the nature of the Church, are both direct and indirect. They didactically assert what the Church is, and they

The Spiritual Nature of the Church

teach such things respecting it, as necessarily lead to a certain conception of its nature.

We may learn from the Bible the true idea of the Church, in the first place, from the use of the word itself. Under all the various applications of the term, that which is essential to the idea will be found to be expressed. In the second place, the equivalent or descriptive terms employed to express the same idea, reveal its nature. In the third place, the attributes ascribed to the Church in the word of God, determine its nature. If those attributes can be affirmed only of a visible society, then the Church must, as to its essence, be such a society. If, on the other hand, they belong only to the communion of saints, then none but saints constitute the Church. These attributes must all be included in the idea of the Church.

They are but different phases or manifestations of its nature. They can all, therefore, be traced back to it, or evolved from it. If the Church is the body of those who are united to Christ by the indwelling of the Holy Spirit, then the indwelling of the Spirit must make the Church holy, visible, perpetual, one, catholic. All these attributes must be referable to that one thing to which the Church owes its nature. In the fourth place, the promises and prerogatives which belong to the Church, teach us very plainly whether it is an external society, or a communion of saints. In the fifth place, there is a necessary connection between a certain scheme of doctrine and a certain theory of the Church. It is admitted that the Church includes all who are in Christ, all who are saints. It is also admitted that all who are in Christ are in the Church. The question, therefore, "Who are in the Church?" must depend upon the answer to the question, "Who are in Christ?" or "How do we become united to him?"

Finally, as the true doctrine concerning the way of salvation leads to the true theory of the Church, we may expect to see that theory asserted and taught in all ages. However corrupted and overlaid it may be, as other doctrines have been, it will be found still preserved and capable of being recognized under all these perversions. The testimony of the Church itself will, therefore, be found to be in favor of the true doctrine as to what the Church is.

The full exposition of these topics would require a treatise by itself. The evidence in favor of the true doctrine concerning the Church, even in the imperfect manner in which it is unfolded in this article, is to be sought through all the following pages, and not exclusively under one particular head. All that is now intended is to present a general view of the principal arguments in support of the doctrine, that the Church consists of saints or true Christians, and that the essential bond of their union is not external organization, but the indwelling of the Holy Ghost.

The Scriptural Use of the Word "Church"

The word *ekklesia*, from *ekkaleo*, *evocare*, means an assembly or body of men evoked, or called out and together.[2] It was used to designate the public assembly of the people, among the Greeks, collected for the transaction of business. It is applied to the tumultuous assembly called together in Ephesus, by the outcries of Demetrius (Acts 19:39). It is used for those who are called out of the world, by the gospel, so as to form a distinct class. It was not the Helotes at Athens who heard the proclamation of the heralds, but the people who actually assembled, who constituted the *ekklesia* of that city. In like manner it is not those who merely hear the call of the gospel, who constitute the Church, but those who obey the call. Thousands of the Jews and Gentiles, in the age of the apostles, heard the gospel, received its invitations, but remained Jews and idolaters. Those only who obeyed the invitation, and separated themselves from their former connections, and entered into a new

---

[2] *Ekklesia* is a Greek word usually translated as "church" or "assembly," *ekkaleo* is Greek for "I call out," and *evocare* is Latin for "to call up."

The Spiritual Nature of the Church

relation and communion, made up the Church of that day. In all the various applications, therefore, of the word *ekklesia* in the New Testament, we find it uniformly used as a collective term for the *kletoi* or *eklektoi*, that is, for those who obey the gospel call, and who are thus selected and separated, as a distinct class from the rest of the world.[3] Sometimes the term includes all who have already, or who shall hereafter accept the call of God. This is the sense of the word in Ephesians 3:10, where it is said to be the purpose of God to manifest unto principalities and powers, by the Church, his manifold wisdom; and in Ephesians 5:25-26, where it is said, that Christ loved the Church and gave himself for it, that he might sanctify and cleanse it with the washing of water by the word; that he might present it to himself a glorious Church, not having spot or wrinkle, or any such thing. Sometimes the word is used for the people of God indefinitely, as when it is said of Paul, he persecuted the Church; or when we are commanded to give no offence to the Church. The word is very commonly used in this sense, as when we speak of the progress of the Church, or pray for the Church. It is not any specific, organized body that is commonly intended in such expressions, but the kingdom of Christ indefinitely. Sometimes it is used for any number of the called, collectively considered, united together by some common bond. Thus we hear of the Church in the house of Priscilla and Aquila, the Church in the house of Nymphas, the Church in the house of Philemon; the Church of Jerusalem, of Antioch, of Corinth, etc. In all these cases, the meaning of the word is the same. It is always used as a collective term for the *kletoi*, either for the whole number, or for any portion of them considered as a whole. The Church of God is the whole number of the elect; the Church of Corinth is the whole number of the called in that city. An organized body may be a Church, and their organization may be the reason for their

---

[3] *Kletoi* is Greek for "called" and *eklektoi* is Greek for "elect."

being considered as a whole or as a unit. But it is not their organization that makes them a Church. The multitude of believers in Corinth, organized or dispersed, is the Church of Corinth, just as the whole multitude of saints in heaven and on earth is the Church of God. It is not organization, but evocation, the actual calling out and separating from others, that makes the Church.

The Church and the Call of God
The nature of the Church, therefore, must depend on the nature of the gospel call. If that call is merely or essentially to the outward profession of certain doctrines, or to baptism, or to any thing external, then the Church must consist of all who make that profession, or are baptized. But if the call of the gospel is to repentance toward God, and faith in our Lord Jesus Christ, then none obey that call but those who repent and believe, and the Church must consist of penitent believers. It cannot require proof that the call of the gospel is to faith and repentance. The great apostle tells us he received his apostleship to the obedience of faith, among all nations, i.e., to bring them to that obedience which consists in faith.[4] He calls those who heard him to witness that he had not failed to testify both to the Jews and also to the Gentiles, repentance toward God, and faith toward our Lord Jesus Christ.[5] No one was admitted by the apostles to the Church, or recognized as of the number of "the called," who did not profess faith and repentance, and such has been the law and practice of the Church ever since. There can, therefore, be no doubt on this subject. What the apostles did, and what all ministers, since their day, have been commissioned to do, is to preach the gospel; to offer men salvation on the condition of faith and repentance. Those who obeyed that call were baptized, and recognized as constituent members of the Church; those who

---

[4] Romans 1:5.
[5] Acts 20:21.

The Spiritual Nature of the Church

rejected it, who refused to repent and believe, were not members, they were not in fact "called," and by that divine vocation[6] separated from the world. It would, therefore, be as unreasonable to call the inhabitants of a country an army, because they heard the call to arms, as to call all who hear but do not obey the gospel, the Church. The army consists of those who actually enroll themselves as soldiers; and the Church consists of those who actually repent and believe, in obedience to the call of the gospel.

This conclusion, to which we are led by the very nature of the call by which the Church is constituted, is confirmed by the unvarying usage of the New Testament. Every *ekklesia* is composed of the *kletoi*, of those called out and assembled. But the word *kletoi*, as applied to Christians, is never used in the New Testament, except in reference to true believers. If, therefore, the Church consists of "the called," it must consist of true believers. That such is the usage of the word "called" in the New Testament, is abundantly evident. In Romans 1:6, believers are designated the *kletoi Iesou Christou*, Christ's called ones. In Romans 8:28, all things are said to work together for good, *tois kata prothesin kletois*, to the called according to purpose. In 1 Corinthians 1:2, 24, we find the same use of the word. The gospel is said to be foolishness to the Greeks, and a stumbling-block to the Jews, but to "the called," it is declared to be the wisdom of God and power of God. The called are distinguished as those to whom the gospel is effectual. Jude addresses believers as the sanctified by the Father, the preserved in Christ Jesus, and "called." In Revelation 17:14, the triumphant followers of the Lamb are called *kletoi kai eklektoi kai pistoi*.[7] The doctrinal usage of the word *kletoi* is, therefore, not a matter of doubt. None but those who truly repent and believe, are ever called *kletoi*, and,

---

[6] i.e., calling.
[7] Greek for "called and elect and faithful."

as the *ekklesia* consists of the *kletoi*, the Church must consist of true believers.

This conclusion is confirmed by a reference to analogous terms applied to believers. As they are *kletoi*, because the subjects of a divine *klesis*, or vocation, so they are *eklektoi* (Romans 8:23; 1 Peter 1:2), *hagiasmenoi* (1 Corinthians 1:2; Jude 1; Hebrews 10:10), *prooristhentes* (Ephesians 1:11), *sodzomenoi* (1 Corinthians 1:18; 2 Corinthians 2:15; 2 Thessalonians 2:11), and *tetagmenoi eis zoen aiaion* (Acts 13:48).[8] All these terms have reference to that divine agency, to that call, choice, separation, or appointment, by which men are made true believers, and they are never applied to any other class.

The use of the cognate words, *kaleo* and *klesis*, goes to confirm the conclusion as to the meaning of the word *kletoi*.[9] When used in reference to the act of God, in calling men by the gospel, they always designate a call that is effectual, so that the subjects of that vocation become the true children of God. Thus, in Romans 8:30, whom he calls, them he also justifies, whom he justifies, them he also glorifies. All the called, therefore, (the *kletoi*, the *ekklesia*) are justified and glorified. In Romans 9:24, the vessels of mercy are said to be those whom God calls. In 1 Corinthians 1:9, believers are said to be called into fellowship of the Son of God. In the same chapter the apostle says: "Ye see your calling, brethren, how that not many wise men after the flesh, not many mighty, not many noble, are *called*," i.e., converted and made the true children of God. In 1 Corinthians 7 the word is used nine times in the same way. In Galatians 1:15, Paul says, speaking of God, "who has called

---

[8] The "called" are here noted by Hodge as being in Scripture called "elect," "sanctified," "predestined," "saved," and "ordained to eternal life." Hodge is continuing his argument that, in scriptural terms, the Church is composed of those who are effectually called by God and are therefore true believers.

[9] Greek for "I call," "calling," and "called," respectively.

The Spiritual Nature of the Church

me by his grace." See also Galatians 5:8, 13; Ephesians 4:4; Colossians 3:15; 1 Thessalonians 2:12, 24; 1 Timothy 6:12; 2 Timothy 1:9. It is said believers are called, not according to their works, but according to the purpose and grace of God given them in Christ Jesus before the world began. In Hebrews 9:5, Christ is said to have died that the called, *hoi keklemenoi*,[10] might receive the eternal inheritance. In 1 Peter 2:9, believers are described as a chosen generation, a royal priesthood, a peculiar people, whom God hath called out of darkness into his marvelous light. In the salutation prefixed to his second Epistle, this apostle wishes all good to those whom God had called by his glorious power.

In proof that the word *klesis* is constantly used in reference to the effectual call of God, see Romans 9:29; 1 Corinthians 1:26; Ephesians 1:18, 4:1; Philippians 3:14; Hebrews 3:1; 2 Peter 1:10.

From these considerations it is clear that the *kletoi*, or "called," are the effectually called, those who really obey the gospel, and by repentance and faith are separated from the world. And as it is admitted that the *ekklesia* is a collective term for the *kletoi*, it follows that none but true believers constitute the Church, or that the Church is the communion of saints. The word in the New Testament is never used except in reference to the company of true believers. This consideration alone is sufficient to determine the nature of the Church.

To this argument it is indeed objected, that as the apostles addressed all the Christians of Antioch, Corinth, or Ephesus, as constituting the Church in those cities, and as among them there were many hypocrites, therefore the word Church designates a body of professors, whether sincere or insincere. The fact is admitted, that all the professors of the true religion in Corinth, without reference to their character, are called the church of Corinth. This, however, is no answer to the preceding argument. It determines nothing as

---

[10] Greek for "those who have been called."

to the nature of the Church. It does not prove it to be an external society, composed of sincere and insincere professors of the true religion. All the professors in Corinth are called saints, sanctified in Christ Jesus, the saved, the children of God, the faithful, believers, etc., etc. Does this prove that there are good and bad saints, holy and unholy sanctified persons, believing and unbelieving believers, or men who are at the same time children of God and children of the devil? Their being called believers does not prove that they were all believers; neither does their being called the Church prove that they were all members of the Church. They are designated according to their profession. In professing to be members of the Church, they professed to be believers, to be saints, and faithful brethren, and this proves that the Church consists of true believers. This will appear more clearly from the following.

Terms Used as Equivalents for the Word "Church"

Those epistles in the New Testament which are addressed to churches, are addressed to believers, saints, the children of God. These latter terms, therefore, are equivalent to the former. The conclusion to be drawn from this fact is, that the Church consists of believers. In the same sense, and in no other, in which infidels may be called believers, and wicked men saints, in the same sense may they be said to be included in the Church. If they are not really believers, they are not the Church. They are not constituent members of the company of believers.

The force of this argument will appear from a reference to the salutations prefixed to these epistles. The epistle to the Romans, for example, is addressed to "the called of Jesus Christ," "the beloved of God," "called to be saints." The epistles to the Corinthians are addressed "to the Church of God which is at Corinth." Who are they? "The sanctified in Christ Jesus, called to be saints," the worshippers of Christ. The Ephesian Church is addressed as "the saints who are in Ephesus, and the faithful in Christ Jesus." The

The Spiritual Nature of the Church

Philippians are called "saints and faithful brethren in Christ." Peter addressed his first Epistle to "the elect according to the foreknowledge of God the Father, through sanctification of the Spirit unto obedience and sprinkling of the blood of Jesus Christ;" i.e., to those who, being elected to obedience and sprinkling of the blood of Jesus, are sanctified by the Spirit. His second Epistle is directed to those who had obtained like precious faith with the apostle himself, through (or in) the righteousness of our God and Savior Jesus Christ.

From this collation it appears, that to call any body of men a Church, is to call them saints, sanctified in Christ Jesus, elected to obedience and sprinkling of the blood of Christ, partakers of the same precious faith with the apostles, the beloved of God, and faithful brethren. The inference from this fact is inevitable. The Church consists of those to whom these terms are applicable.

The only way by which this argument can be evaded is, by saying that the faith here spoken of is mere speculative faith, the sanctification intended is mere external consecration, and the sonship referred to, is merely adoption to external privileges, or a church state. This objection, however, is completely obviated by the contents of these epistles. The persons to whom these terms are applied, and who are represented as constituting the Church, are described as really holy in heart and life; not mere professors of the true faith, but true believers; not merely the recipients of certain privileges, but the children of God and heirs of eternal life.

New Testament Churches Are Composed of Believers

The members of the Church in Corinth are declared to be in fellowship with Jesus Christ, chosen of God, inhabited by his Spirit, washed, sanctified, and justified in the name of the Lord Jesus, and by the Spirit of our God. That the faith which Paul attributes to the members of the Church in Rome, and the sonship of which he represents them as partakers, were not speculative or external, is evident, because he says, those who believe have peace with God, rejoice in hope of his glory and have his love shed abroad in their hearts. Those who are in Christ, he says, are not only free from condemnation, but walk after the Spirit, and are spiritually minded. Being the sons of God, they are led by the Spirit, they have the spirit of adoption, and are joint heirs with Jesus Christ of a heavenly inheritance. The members of the Church in Ephesus were faithful brethren in Christ Jesus, sealed with the Holy Spirit of promise, quickened and raised from spiritual death, and made to sit in heavenly places. All those in Colossae who are designated as the Church, are described as reconciled unto God, the recipients of Christ, who were complete in him, all whose sins are pardoned. The Church in Thessalonica consisted of those whose work of faith, and labor of love, and patience of hope, Paul joyfully remembered, and of whose election of God he was well assured. They were children of the light and of the day, whom God had appointed to the obtaining of salvation through our Lord Jesus Christ. The churches to whom Peter wrote consisted of those who had been begotten again to a lively hope, by the resurrection of Christ from the dead. Though they had not seen the Savior, they loved him, and believing on him, rejoiced with joy unspeakable and full of glory. They had purified their souls unto unfeigned love of the brethren, having been born again, not of corruptible seed, but of incorruptible, by the word of God. Those whom John recognized as members of the Church he says had received an anointing of the Holy one, which abode with them, teaching them the truth. They were the sons of God, who had overcome the world, who believing in Christ had eternal life.

From all this, it is evident that the terms, believers, saints, children of God, the sanctified, the justified, and the like, are equivalent to the collective term Church, so that any company of men addressed as a Church, are always addressed as saints, faithful

The Spiritual Nature of the Church

brethren, partakers of the Holy Ghost, and children of God. The Church, therefore, consists exclusively of such. That these terms do not express merely a professed faith or external consecration is evident, because those to whom they are applied are declared to be no longer unjust, extortioners, thieves, drunkards, covetous, revilers, or adulterers, but to be led by the Spirit to the belief and obedience of the truth. The Church, therefore, consists of believers; and if it consists of believers, it consists of those who have peace with God, and have overcome the world.

It is not to be inferred from the fact that all the members of the Christian societies in Rome, Corinth, and Ephesus, are addressed as believers, that they all had true faith. But we can infer, that since what is said of them is said of them as believers, it had no application to those who were without faith. In like manner, though all are addressed as belonging to the Church, what is said of the Church had no application to those who were not really its members. Addressing a body of professed believers, as believers, does not prove them to be all sincere; neither does addressing a body of men as a Church, prove that they all belong to the Church. In both cases they are addressed according to their profession. If it is a fatal error to transfer what is said in Scripture of believers, to mere professors, to apply to nominal what is said of true Christians, it is no less fatal to apply what is said of the Church to those who are only by profession its members. It is no more proper to infer that the Church consists of the promiscuous multitude of sincere and insincere professors of the true faith, from the fact that all the professors, good and bad, in Corinth, are called the Church, than it would be to infer that they were all saints and children of God, because they are all so denominated. It is enough to determine the true nature of the Church, that none are ever addressed as its members, who are not, at the same time, addressed as true saints and sincere believers.

The Church and the Lord's Supper

Descriptions of the Church

The descriptions of the Church given in the word of God, apply to none but true believers, and therefore true believers constitute the Church. These descriptions relate either to the relation which the Church sustains to Christ, or to the character of its members, or to its future destiny. The argument is that none but true believers bear that relation to Christ which the Church is said to sustain to him; none but believers possess the character ascribed to members of the Church; and none but believers are heirs of those blessings which are in reserve for the Church. If all this is so, it follows that the Church consists of those who truly believe. It will not be necessary to keep these points distinct, because in many passages of Scripture, the relation which the Church bears to Christ, the character of its members, and its destiny, are all brought into view.

The Body of Christ
The Church is described as the body of Christ (Ephesians 1:22, 4:15, 16; Colossians 1:18). The relation expressed by this designation includes subjection, dependence, and participation of the same life, sympathy, and community. Those who are the body of Christ are dependent upon him and subject to him, as the human body to its head. They are partakers of his life. The human body is animated by one soul, and has one vital principle. This is the precise truth which the Scriptures teach in reference to the Church as the body of Christ. It is his body, because animated by his Spirit, so that if any man have not the Spirit of Christ, he is none of his (Romans 8:9), for it is by one Spirit we are all baptized into one body (1 Corinthians 12:13). The distinguishing characteristic of the members of Christ's body, is the indwelling of the Holy Ghost. They are therefore called *pneumatikoi*, men having the Spirit. They are led by the Spirit. They are spiritually minded. All this is true of sincere believers alone. It is not true of the promiscuous body of professors, nor of the members of any visible society, as such, and

therefore no such visible society is the body of Christ. What is said of the body of Christ, is not true of any external organized corporation on earth, and, therefore, the two cannot be identical.

Again, as the body sympathizes with the head, and the members sympathize one with another, so all the members of Christ's body sympathize with him, and with each other. This sympathy is not merely a duty, it is a fact. Where it does not exist, there membership in Christ's body does not exist. All, therefore, who are members of Christ's body feel his glory to be their own, his triumph to be their victory. They love those whom he loves, and they hate what he hates. Finally, as the human head and body have a common destiny, so have Christ and his Church. As it partakes of his life, it shall participate in his glory. The members of his body suffer with him here, and shall reign with him hereafter.

It is to degrade and destroy the gospel to apply this description of the Church as the body of Christ, to the mass of nominal Christians, the visible Church, which consists of "all sorts of men." No such visible society is animated by his Spirit, is a partaker of his life, and heir of his glory. It is to obliterate the distinction between holiness and sin, between the Church and the world, between the children of God and the children of the devil, to apply what the Bible says of the body of Christ to any promiscuous society of saints and sinners.

The Temple of God

The Church is declared to be the temple of God, because he dwells in it by his Spirit. That temple is composed of living stones (1 Peter 2:4, 5). "Know ye not," says the apostle to the Corinthians, "that your body is the temple of the Holy Ghost, which is in you?" (1 Corinthians 6:19). The inference from this description of the Church is, that it is composed of those in whom the Spirit of God dwells; but the Spirit of God dwells only in true believers, and therefore the Church consists of such believers.

The Family of God
The Church is the family of God. Those, therefore, who are not the children of God are not members of his Church. The wicked are declared to be the children of the devil; they therefore cannot be the children of God. Those only are his children who have the spirit of adoption; and being children, are heirs of God and joint heirs with Christ (Romans 8:16, 17).

The Flock of Christ
The Church is the flock of Christ; its members are his sheep. He knows them, leads them, feeds them, and lays down his life for them. They were given to him by the Father, and no one is able to pluck them out of his hand. They know his voice and follow him, but a stranger they will not follow (John 10). This description of the Church as the flock of Christ, is applicable only to saints or true believers, and therefore they alone constitute his Church.

The Bride of Christ
The Church is the bride of Christ; the object of his peculiar love, for which he gave himself, that he might present it to himself a glorious Church, not having spot or wrinkle or any such thing. No man, saith the Scripture, ever yet hated his own flesh but nourisheth and cherisheth it, even as the Lord the Church (Ephesians 5:25–30). It is not true, according to the Bible, that any but true Christians are the objects of this peculiar love of Christ, and therefore they alone constitute that Church which is his bride.

According to the Scriptures, then, the Church consists of those who are in Christ, to whom he is made wisdom, righteousness, sanctification, and redemption; of those who are his body, in whom he dwells by his Spirit; of those who are the family of God,

The Spiritual Nature of the Church

the children of his grace; of those who, as living stones, compose that temple in which God dwells, and who rest on that elect, tried, precious corner-stone, which God has laid in Zion; of those who are the bride of Christ, purchased by his blood, sanctified by his word, sacraments, and Spirit, to be presented at last before the presence of his glory with exceeding joy. These descriptions of the Church are inapplicable to any external visible society as such; to the Church of Rome, the Church of England, or the Presbyterian Church. The only Church of which these things are true, is the communion of saints, the body of true Christians.

The Attributes of the Church

The great question at issue on this whole subject is, whether we are to conceive of the Church, in its essential character, as an external society, or as the communion of saints. One method of deciding this question is by a reference to the acknowledged attributes of the Church. If those attributes belong only to a visible society, then the Church must be such a society. But if they can be predicated only of the communion of saints, then the Church is a spiritual body and not an external, visible society.

The Church is the body of Christ, in which he dwells by his Spirit. It is in virtue of this indwelling of the Spirit, that the Church is what she is, and all that she is. To this source her holiness, unity, and perpetuity, are to be referred, and under these attributes all others are comprehended.

Holiness

First, then, as to holiness. The Church considered as the communion of saints is holy. Where the Spirit of God is, there is holiness. If, therefore, the Spirit dwells in the Church, the Church must be holy, not merely nominally, but really; not merely because her founder, her doctrines, her institutions are holy, but because her members are personally holy. They are, and must be, holy brethren, saints, the sanctified in Christ Jesus, beloved of God. They are led by the Spirit, and mind the things of the Spirit. The indwelling of the Spirit produces this personal holiness, and that separation from the world and consecration to God, which make the Church a holy nation, a peculiar people, zealous of good works. The Church is defined to be a company of believers, the *coetus fidelium*.[11] To say that the Church is holy, is to say that that company of men and women who compose the Church, is holy. It is a contradiction to say that "all sorts of men," thieves, murderers, drunkards, the unjust, the rapacious, and the covetous, enter into the composition of a society whose essential attribute is holiness. To say that a man is unjust is to say that he is not holy, and to say that he is not holy is to say that he is not one of a company of saints. If then we conceive of the Church as the communion of saints, as the body of Christ, in which the Holy Spirit dwells as the source of its life, we see that the Church is and must be holy. It must be inwardly pure, that is, its members must be regenerated men, and it must be really separated from the world, and consecrated to God. These are the two ideas included in the scriptural sense of holiness, and in both these senses the Church is truly holy. But in neither sense can holiness be predicated of any external visible society as such. No such society is really pure, nor is it really separated from the world, and devoted to God. This is evident from the most superficial observation. It is plain that neither the Roman, the Greek, the English, nor the Presbyterian Church, falls within the definition of the Church, as the *coetus sanctorum*,[12] or company of believers. No one of these societies is holy, they are all more or less corrupt and worldly. Their church state does not in the least depend on the moral character of their members, if the Church is essentially an

---

[11] Latin for "community of the faithful."
[12] Latin for "community of the holy."

The Spiritual Nature of the Church

external society. Such a society may sink to the lowest degree of corruption, and yet be a church, provided it retain its external integrity. Of no such a society, however, is holiness an attribute, and all history and daily observation concur in their testimony as to this fact. If, therefore, no community of which holiness is not an attribute can be the Church, it follows, that no external society, composed of "all sorts of men," can be the holy, catholic Church. Those, therefore, who regard the Church as an external society, are forced to deny that the Church is holy. They all assert that it is composed of hypocrites and unrenewed men, as well as of saints. Thus, for example, Bellarmine defines the Church to be "the society of men united by the profession of the same Christian faith, and the communion of the same sacraments, under the government of legitimate pastors, and especially of the only vicar of Christ here on earth, the Roman Pontiff."[13] By the first clause of this definition he excludes all who do not profess the true faith, such as Jews, Mohammedans, Pagans, and heretics; by the second, all the unbaptized and the excommunicated; by the third, all schismatics, i.e., all who do not submit to legitimate pastors (prelates), especially to the Pope. All other classes of men, he adds, are included in the Church, *etiamsi reprobi, scelesti et impii sint.*[14] The main point of difference between the Romish and Protestant theories of the Church, he says, is that the latter requires internal virtues in order to Church membership, but the former requires nothing beyond outward profession, for the Church, he adds, is just as much an external society as the Roman people, the kingdom of France, or the republic of Venice.[15]

---

[13] Robert Bellarmine (1542-1621) was one of the most significant defenders of Roman Catholicism during the Catholic Counter Reformation. The reference information Hodge provides for this quote is "Lib. III. c. ii, col. 108."

[14] Latin for "even if they should be fallen, wicked, and impious."

[15] The reference information provided here is "Ibid., col. 109."

The Oxford theory of the Church differs from the Romish only in excluding subjection to the Pope as one of its essential characteristics. The Church is defined to be "The whole society of Christians throughout the world, including all those who profess their belief in Christ, and who are subject to lawful pastors."[16] By Christians, in this definition, are meant nominal, or professed Christians. According to this view, neither "inward regeneration, nor visible sanctity of life, is requisite for admission to the Church of Christ." "The Scriptures and the universal Church appoint," it is said, "only one mode in which Christians are to be made members of the Church. It is baptism, which renders us, by divine right, members of the Church, and entitles us to all the privileges of the faithful."[17] Again, when speaking of baptism, which thus secures a divine right to all the privileges of the faithful, it is said, there is no "mention of regeneration, sanctity, real piety, visible or invisible, as prerequisite to its reception."[18] Holiness, therefore, is denied to be an attribute of the Church in any proper sense of the term. This denial is the unavoidable consequence of regarding the Church as a visible society, analogous to an earthly kingdom. As holiness is not necessary to citizenship in the kingdom of Spain, or republic of Venice, holiness is not an attribute of either of those communities. Neither Spain nor Venice is, as such, holy. And if the Church, in its true essential character, be a visible society, of which men become members by mere profession, and without holiness, then holiness is not an attribute of the Church. But, as by common consent the Church is holy, a theory of its nature which excludes this attribute, must be both unscriptural and uncatholic, and therefore false.

---

[16] William Palmer, *A Treatise on the Church of Christ*, 2 vols. (London: J. G. & F. Rivington, 1838), 1:4.
[17] Palmer, *Treatise on the Church*, 1:140.
[18] Palmer, *Treatise on the Church*, 1:410.

The Spiritual Nature of the Church

No false theory can be consistent. If, therefore, the theory of the Church which represents it as an external society of professors, is false, we may expect to see its advocates falling continually into suicidal contradictions. The whole Romish or ritual system is founded on the assumption, that the attributes and prerogatives ascribed in Scripture to the Church, belong to the visible Church, irrespective of the character of its members. Nothing is required for admission into that society, but profession of its faith, reception of its sacraments, and submission to its legitimate rulers. If a whole nation of Pagans or Mohammedans should submit to these external conditions, they would be true members of the Church, though ignorant of its doctrines, though destitute of faith, and sunk in moral corruption. To this society the attributes of holiness, unity, and perpetuity belong; this society, thus constituted of "all sorts of men," has the prerogative authoritatively to teach, and to bind and loose; and the teaching and discipline of this society, Christ has promised to ratify in heaven. The absurdities and enormities, however, which flow from this theory, are so glaring and atrocious, that few of its advocates have the nerve to look them in the face. As we have seen, it is a contradiction to call a society composed of "all sorts of men" holy. Those who teach, therefore, that the Church is such a society, sometimes say that holiness is not a condition of membership; in other words, is not an attribute of the Church; and sometimes, that none but the holy are really in the Church, that the wicked are not its true members. But, if this be so, as holiness has its seat in the heart, no man can tell certainly who are holy, and therefore no one can tell who are the real members of the Church, or who actually constitute the body of Christ, which we are required to join and to obey. The Church, therefore, if it consists only of the holy, is not an external society, and the whole ritual system falls to the ground.

Neither Romish nor Anglican writers can escape from these contradictions. Augustine says the Church is a living body, in which there are both a soul and body. Some members are of the Church in both respects, being united to Christ, as well externally as internally. These are the living members of the Church; others are of the soul, but not of the body—that is, they have faith and love, without external communion with the Church. Others, again, are of the body and not of the soul—that is, they have no true faith. These last, he says, are as the hairs, or nails, or evil humors of the human body.[19] According to Augustine, then, the wicked are not true members of the Church; their relation to it is altogether external. They no more make up the Church, than the scurf or hair on the surface of the skin make up the human body. This representation is in entire accordance with the Protestant doctrine, that the Church is a communion of saints, and that none hut the holy are its true members. It expressly contradicts the Romish and Oxford theory, that the Church consists of all sorts of men; and that the baptized, no matter what their character, if they submit to their legitimate pastors, are by divine right constituent portions of the Church; and that none who do not receive the sacraments, and who are not thus subject, can be members of the body of Christ. Yet this doctrine of Augustine, so inconsistent with their own, is conceded by Romish writers. They speak of the relation of the wicked to the Church as merely external or nominal, as a dead branch to a tree, or as chaff to the wheat. So, also, does Mr. Palmer, who says: "It is generally allowed that the wicked belong only externally to the Church."[20] Again: "That the ungodly, whether secret or manifest, do not really belong to the Church, considered as to its invisible character—namely, as consisting of its essential and permanent members, the elect, predestinated, and

---

[19] The reference Hodge provides here is "In Breviculo Collationis. Collat. iii."
[20] Palmer, *Treatise on the Church*, 4.

sanctified, who are known to God only, I admit."[21] That is, he admits his whole theory to be untenable. He admits, after all, that the wicked "do not really belong to the Church," and therefore, that the real or true Church consists of the sanctified in Christ Jesus. What is said of the wheat is surely not true of the chaff; and what the Bible says of the Church is not true of the wicked. Yet all Romanism, all ritualism, rests on the assumption, that what is said of the wheat is true of the chaff—that what is said of the communion of saints, is true of a body composed of all sorts of men. The argument, then, here is that as holiness is an attribute of the Church, no body which is not holy can be the Church. No external visible society, as such, is holy; and, therefore, the Church, of which the Scriptures speak, is not a visible society, but the communion of saints.

Spiritual Unity
The same argument may be drawn from the other attributes of the Church. It is conceded that unity is one of its essential attributes. The Church is one, as there is, and can be but one body of Christ. The Church as the communion of saints is one; as an external society it is not one; therefore, the Church is the company of believers, and not an external society.

The unity of the Church is threefold: 1. Spiritual, the unity of faith and of communion, 2. Comprehensive; the Church is one as it is catholic, embracing all the people of God, and 3. Historical; it is the same Church in all ages. In all these senses, the Church considered as the communion of saints, is one; in no one of these senses can unity be predicated of the
Church as visible.

The Church, considered as the communion of saints, is one in faith. The Spirit of God leads his people into all truth. He takes of

---

[21] Palmer, *Treatise on the Church*, 139.

the things of Christ and shows them unto them. They are all taught of God. The anointing which they have received abideth with them, and teacheth them all things, and is truth (1 John 2:27). Under this teaching of the Spirit, which is promised to all believers, and which is with and by the word, they are all led to the knowledge and belief of all necessary truth. And within the limits of such necessary truths, all true Christians, the whole *coetus sanctorum*, or body of believers, are one. In all ages and in all nations, wherever there are true Christians, you find they have, as to all essential matters, one and the same faith.

The Holy Ghost is the spirit of love as well as of truth, and therefore all those in whom he dwells are one in affection as well as in faith. They have the same inward experience, the same conviction of sin, the same repentance toward God and faith in our Lord Jesus Christ, the same love of holiness, and desire after conformity to the image of God. There is, therefore, an inward fellowship or congeniality between them, which proves them to be one Spirit. They all stand in the same relation to God and Christ; they constitute one family, of which God is the Father; one kingdom, of which Christ is the Lord. They have a common interest and common expectation. The triumph of the Redeemer's kingdom is the common joy and triumph of all his people. They have, therefore, the fellowship which belongs to the subjects of the same king, to the children of the same family, and to the members of the same body. If one member suffers, all the members suffer with it; and if one member rejoices, all the members rejoice with it. This sympathy is an essential characteristic of the body of Christ. Those who do not possess this affection and fellow-feeling for his members, are none of his. This inward spiritual communion expresses itself outwardly, not only in acts of kindness, but especially and appropriately in all acts of Christian fellowship. True believers are disposed to recognize each other as such, to unite as Christians in the service of their common Lord, and to make one joint profession

The Spiritual Nature of the Church

before the world of their allegiance to him. In this, the highest and truest sense, the Church is one. It is one body in Christ Jesus. He dwells by his Spirit in all his members, and thus unites them as one living whole, leading all to the belief of the same truths, and binding all in the bond of peace. This is the unity of which the apostle speaks: "There is one body and one Spirit, even as ye are called in one hope of your calling; one Lord, one faith, one baptism, one God and Father of all, who is above all, and through all, and in you all" (Ephesians 4:4-6). Such is the unity which belongs to the Church; it does not belong to any external society, and therefore no such society can be the Church to which the attributes and prerogatives of the body of Christ belong.

In proof that spiritual unity cannot be predicated of the external Church, it is sufficient to refer to the obvious fact that the Holy Spirit, the ground and bond of that unity, does not dwell in all the members of that Church. Wherever he dwells there are the fruits of holiness, and as those fruits are not found in all who profess to be Christians, the Spirit does not dwell in them so as to unite them to the body of Christ. The consequence is, they have neither the unity of faith nor of communion.

As to the unity of faith, it is undeniable that all Christian societies do not even profess the same faith. While all unite in certain doctrines, they each profess or deny what the others regard as fatal error or necessary truth. The Greek, Latin, and Protestant Churches do not regard themselves as one in faith. Each declares the others to be heretical. But this is not all. Unity of faith does not exist within the pale of these several churches. In each of them all grades and kinds of doctrine, from atheism to orthodoxy, are entertained. No one doubts this. It would be preposterous to assert that all the members of the Latin Church hold the public faith of that society. The great body of them do not know what that faith is, and multitudes among them are infidels. Neither can any one pretend that the standards of the English, Dutch, or Prussian

Church, express the faith of all their members. It is a notorious and admitted fact that every form of religious faith and infidelity is to be found among the members of those societies. Unity of faith, therefore, is one of the attributes of the true Church, which, with no show of truth or reason, can be predicated of any external society calling itself the Church of God.

The case is no less plain with regard to communion. The societies constituting the visible Church, do not maintain Christian communion. They do not all recognize each other as brethren, nor do they unite in the offices of Christian worship and fellowship. On the contrary, they, in many cases, mutually excommunicate each other. The Greek, Latin, and Protestant Churches, each stands aloof. They are separate communions, having no ecclesiastical fellowship whatever. This kind of separation, however, is not so entirely inconsistent with the communion of saints, as the absence of brotherly love, and the presence of all unholy affections, which characterize to so great an extent these nominal Christians. If it be true that there is a warm sympathy, a real brotherly affection, between all the members of Christ's body, then nothing can be plainer than that the great mass of nominal Christians are not members of that body. The unity of the Spirit, the bond of perfectness, true Christian love, does not unite the members of any extended visible society into one holy brotherhood; and therefore no such society is the Church of Christ.

Romanists answer this argument by vehement assertion. They first degrade the idea of unity into that of outward connection. So that men profess the same faith, they are united in faith, even though many of them be heretics or infidels. If they receive the same sacraments and submit to the same rulers, they are in Christian communion, even though they bite and devour one another. They, then, boldly assert that the Church is confined to themselves; that Greeks, Anglicans, Lutherans, and Reformed, are out of the Church. To make it appear that the Church, in their view of its

The Spiritual Nature of the Church

nature, is one in faith and in communion, they deny that any body of men, or any individual, belongs to the Church, who does not profess their faith and submit to their discipline. Thus even the false, deteriorated idea of unity, which they claim, can be predicated of the Church only by denying the Christian name to more than one half of Christendom.

The answer given to this argument by Anglicans of the Oxford school, is still less satisfactory. They admit that the Church is one in faith and communion, that either heresy or schism is destructive of all saving connection with the body of Christ. To all appearance, however, the Church of England does not hold the faith of the Church of Rome, nor is she in ecclesiastical communion with her Latin sister. She is also almost as widely separated from the Greek and Oriental Churches. How low must the idea of unity be brought down, to make it embrace all these conflicting bodies! The Oxford writers, therefore, in order to save their church standing, are obliged, first, to teach with Rome that unity of the Church is merely in appearance or profession; secondly, that England and Rome do not differ as to matters of faith; and, thirdly, that notwithstanding their mutual denunciations, and, on the part of Rome, of the most formal act of excommunication, they are still in communion. The unity of communion therefore, is, according to their doctrine, compatible with non-communion and mutual excommunication. It is, however, a contradiction in terms, to assert that the Churches of Rome and England, in a state of absolute schism in reference to each other, are yet one in faith and communion. The essential attribute of unity, therefore, cannot be predicated of the external Church, either as to doctrine or as to fellowship.

The Unity of Catholicity

The second form of unity is catholicity. The Church is one because it embraces all the people of God. This was the prominent idea of unity in the early centuries of the Christian era. The Church is one, because there is none other. Those out of the Church are, therefore, out of Christ; they are not members of his body, nor partakers of his Spirit. This is the universal faith of Christendom. All denominations, in all ages, have, agreeably to the plain teaching of the Scriptures, and the very nature of the gospel, maintained that there is no salvation out of the Church; in other words, that the Church is catholic, embracing all the people of God in all parts of the world. Of course it depends on our idea of the Church, whether this attribute of comprehensive unity belongs to it or not. If the Church is essentially a visible monarchical society, of which the Bishop of Rome is the head, then there can be no true religion and no salvation out of the pale of that society. To admit the possibility of men being saved who are not subject to the Pope, is to admit that they can be saved out of the Church; and to say they can be saved out of the Church, is to say they can be saved out of Christ, which no Christians admit. If the Church is a visible aristocratical society, under the government of prelates having succession, then the unity of the Church implies, that that those only who are subject to such prelates are within its pale. There can, therefore, be neither true religion nor salvation except among prelatists. This is a conclusion which flows unavoidably from the idea of the Church as an external visible society. Neither Romanists nor Anglicans [of the Oxford School] shrink from this conclusion. They avow the premises and the inevitable sequence. Mr. Palmer says: "It is not, indeed, to be supposed or believed for a moment that divine grace would permit the really holy and justified members of Christ to fall from the way of life. He would only permit the unsanctified, the enemies of Christ, to sever themselves from that fountain where his Spirit is given freely."[22] This he says in commenting on a dictum of Augustine, "Let us hold it as a thing unshaken and firm,

---

[22] Palmer, *Treatise on the Church*, 1:54.

The Spiritual Nature of the Church

that no good men can divide themselves from the Church."[23] He further quotes Irenaeus, as saying that God has placed every operation of his Spirit in the Church, so that none have the Spirit but those who are in the Church, "for where the Church is, there is the Spirit of God; and where the Spirit of God is, there also the Church and every grace exist."[24] Cyprian is urged as another authority, who says: "Whosoever, divorced from the Church, is united to an adulteress, is separated from the Church's promises; nor shall that man attain the rewards of Christ, who relinquishes his Church. He is a stranger, he is profane, he is an enemy."[25] All this is undoubtedly true. It is true, as Augustine says, that the good cannot divide themselves from the Church; it is true, as Irenaeus says, where the Church is, there the Spirit of God is; and where the Spirit is, there the Church is. This is the favorite motto of Protestants. It is also true, as Cyprian says, that he who is separated from the Church, is separated from Christ. This brings the nature of the Church down to a palpable matter of fact. Are there any fruits of the Spirit, any repentance, faith, and holy living, among those who do not obey the Pope? If so, then the Church is not a monarchy of which the Pope is the head. Is there any true religion, are there any of the people of God who are not subject to prelates? If so, then the Church is not a society subject to bishops having succession. These are questions which can be easily answered. It is, indeed, impossible, in every particular case, to discriminate between true and false professors of religion; but still, as a class, we can distinguish good men from bad men, the children of God from the children of this world. Men do not gather grapes of thorns, nor figs of thistles. By their fruit we can know them. A wolf may indeed at times appear in sheep's clothing; nevertheless, men can distinguish sheep from

---

[23] *Adv. Parmenian*, Lib. iii. ch. 5.
[24] *Adv. Haeres*, iii. 24, p. 223.
[25] *De Unitate*, p. 254.

wolves. We can therefore determine, with full assurance, whether it is true, as the Romish theory of the Church requires, that there is no religion among Protestants, whether all the seemingly pious men of the English Church, for example, are mere hypocrites. This is a question about which no rational man has any doubt, and, therefore, we see not how any such man can fail to see that the Romish theory of the Church is false. It is contradicted by notorious facts. With like assurance we decide against the [High Church] Anglican theory, because if that theory is true, then there is no religion, and never has been any, out of the pale of the Episcopal Church. It is, however, equivalent to a confession that we ourselves are destitute of the Spirit of Christ, to refuse to recognize as his people the thousands of Presbyterians, Lutherans, and Reformed, who have lived for his service, and died to his glory. Here the ritual theory of the Church breaks down entirely. If the Church is an external society, that society must include all good men, all the children of God in the world. No such society does embrace all such men, and, therefore, the Church is not a visible society. It is a communion of saints. The very fact that a man is a saint, a child of God that is born of the Spirit, makes him a member of the Church. To say, therefore, with Augustine, that no good man can leave the Church, is only to say that the good will love and cleave to each other; to say, with Irenaeus, that where the Spirit of God is, there is the Church, is to say the presence of the Spirit makes the Church; and to say with Cyprian, that he who is separated from the Church, is separated from Christ, is only saying, that if a man love not his brother whom he hath seen, he cannot love God whom he hath not seen. If the Church is the communion of saints, it includes all saints; it has catholic unity because it embraces all the children of God. And to say there is no salvation out of the Church, in this sense of the word, is only saying there is no salvation for the wicked, for the unrenewed and unsanctified. But to say there is no piety and no salvation out of the papal or prelatic

The Spiritual Nature of the Church

Church, is very much like doing despite unto the Spirit of God; it is to say of multitudes of true Christians, what the Pharisees said of our Lord; "They cast out devils by Beelzebub, the chief of devils."[26] That is, it is denying the well authenticated work of the Spirit, and attributing to some other and some evil source, what is really the operation of the Holy Ghost. Wherever the Spirit of God is, there the Church is; and as the Spirit is not only within, but without all external church organizations, so the Church itself cannot be limited to any visible society.

The Historical Unity of the Church
The historical unity of the Church is its perpetuity; its remaining one and the same in all ages. In this sense, also, the true Church is one. It is now what it was in the days of the apostles. It has continued the same without interruption, from the beginning, and is to continue until the final consummation; for the gates of hell can never prevail against it. About this there is no dispute; all Christians admit the Church to be in this sense perpetual. In asserting the historical unity, or uninterrupted continuance of the Church, all must maintain the unbroken continuance of every thing which, according to their several theories, is essential to its existence. If the Church is a visible society, professing the true faith, and subject to lawful prelates, and especially to the Pope of Rome, then the perpetuity of the Church supposes the continued existence of such a society, thus organized, always professing the true faith, and always subject to its lawful rulers. There must therefore, always be an external visible society; that society must profess the truth; there must always be prelates legitimately consecrated, and a lawful pope. If, according to the Anglican theory, the Church is precisely what Romanists declare it to be, except subjection to the

---

[26] Cf. Matthew 12:24.

pope, then its perpetuity involves all the particulars above mentioned, except the continued recognition of the headship of the bishop of Rome. If, on the other hand, the Church is a company of believers, if it is the communion of saints, all that is essential to its perpetuity is that there should always be believers. It is not necessary they should be externally organized, much less is it necessary that they should be organized in any prescribed form. It is not necessary that any line of officers should be uninterruptedly continued; much less is it necessary that those officers should be prelates or popes. All that God has promised, and all that we have a right to expect, is, that the true worshippers of the Lord Jesus shall never entirely fail. They may be few and scattered; they may be even unknown to each other, and, in a great measure, to the world; they may be as the seven thousand in the days of the prophet Elijah, who had not bowed the knee unto Baal; still, so long as they exist, the Church, considered as the communion of saints, the mystical body of Christ on earth, continues to exist.

The argument from this source, in favor of the Protestant theory of the Church, is that in no other sense is the Church perpetual. No existing external society has continued uninterruptedly to profess the true faith. Rome was at one time Arian, at another Pelagian, at another, according to the judgment of the Church of England, idolatrous. All Latin churches were subject to the instability of the Church of Rome. No existing Eastern Church has continued the same in its doctrines, from the times of the apostles to the present time. That there has been an interrupted succession of popes and prelates validly consecrated, is admitted to be a matter of faith, and not of sight. From the nature of the case it does not admit of historical proof. The chances, humanly speaking, are as a million to one against it. If it is assumed, it must be on the ground of the supposed necessity of such succession to the perpetuity of the Church, which is a matter of promise. But the Church can exist without a pope, without prelates, yea, without presbyters, if in its

The Spiritual Nature of the Church

essential nature it is the communion of saints. There is, therefore, no promise of an uninterrupted succession of validly ordained church-officers, and consequently no foundation for faith in any such succession. In the absence of any such promise, the historical argument against "apostolic succession," becomes overwhelming and unanswerable.

We must allow the attributes of the Church to determine our conception of its nature. If no external society is perpetual; if every existing visible Church has more than once apostatized from the faith, then the Church must be something which can continue in the midst of the general defection of all external societies; then external organization is not essential to the Church, much less can any particular mode of organization be essential to its existence. The only Church which is holy, which is one, which is catholic, apostolic, and perpetual, is the communion of saints, the company of faithful men, the mystical body of Christ, whose only essential bond of union is the indwelling of the Holy Ghost. That Spirit, however, always produces faith and love, so that all in whom he dwells are united in faith and Christian fellowship. And as, in virtue of the divine promise, the Spirit is to remain constantly gathering in the people of God, until Christ comes the second time, so the Church can never fail. The attributes, then, of holiness, unity, and perpetuity, do not belong to any external society, and therefore no such society can be the Church. They are all found, in their strictest sense and highest measure, in the communion of saints, and therefore, the saints constitute the one, holy, apostolic, Catholic Church.

The Promises and Prerogatives of the Church

The Scriptures abound with promises addressed to the Church, and they ascribe certain prerogatives to it. From the character of these promises and prerogatives, we may infer the nature of the Church.

The Promise of Christ's Presence to the Church
The most comprehensive of the promises in question is that of the continued presence of Christ, by the indwelling of his Spirit. This promise is often given in express terms, and is involved in the description of the Church as the body of Christ and the temple of God. It is not his body, neither is it the temple of God, without the presence of the Spirit. The presence of God is not inoperative. It is like the presence of light and heat, or of knowledge and love, which of necessity manifest themselves by their effects. In like manner, and by a like necessity, the presence of God is manifested by holiness, righteousness, and peace. He is not, where these graces are not; just as certainly as light is not present in the midst of darkness. The promise of God to his Church is, "Lo, I am with you always," in every age and in every part of the world; so that where the Spirit of God is, there is the Church; and where the Church is, there is the Spirit. The presence promised is, therefore, a perpetual presence. It is also universal. God does not promise to be with the officers of the Church to the exclusion of the members; nor with some members to the exclusion of others. The soul is not in the head of the human body, to the exclusion of the limbs; nor is it in the eyes and ears, to the exclusion of the hands or feet. So long as it is in the body at all, it is in the whole body. In like manner the promised presence of God with his Church relates to all its members.

If this is so, if God has promised to be with his Church; if his presence is operative; if it is perpetual and all-pervading, then it is plain that this promise was never made to any external society, for to no such society has it ever been fulfilled. No such society has had the persistency in truth and holiness, which the divine presence of necessity secures. If in one age it professes the truth, in another it professes error. If at one time its members appear holy, at another they are most manifestly corrupt. Or, if some manifest the presence of the Spirit, others give evidence that they are not under his influence. It is, therefore, just as plain that God is not always present with the external Church, as that the sun is not always above our horizon. The nominal Church would correspond with the real, the visible with the invisible, if the promise of the divine presence belonged to the former. With his own people God is always present; they, therefore, must constitute that Church to whom the promise of his presence belongs.

The Promise of Divine Teaching to the Church
The promise of divine teaching is made to the Church. This is included in the promise of the Holy Spirit, who is the Spirit of truth, the source of light and knowledge, wherever he dwells. Christ, when about to leave the world, promised his disciples that he would send them the Spirit, to guide them into all truth. With regard to this promise it is to be remarked, 1. That it is made to all the members of the Church. It is not the peculium of its officers, for it is expressly said, "Ye shall be all taught of God."[27] And the apostle John says to all believers, "Ye have an unction from the Holy One, and ye know all things."[28] 2. It relates only to necessary truths. God has not promised to teach his people all science, nor has he promised to render them infallible in matters of religion. All he has promised, is to teach them whatever is necessary to their salvation, and to qualify them for the work to which they are called. 3. This divine teaching is effectual and abiding. "The anointing," says the apostle, "which ye have received of him, abideth with you."[29] Those who are taught of God, therefore, continue in the knowledge and acknowledgment of the truth.

---

[27] John 6:45.
[28] 1 John 2:20.
[29] 1 John 2:27.

The Church and the Lord's Supper

That such divine teaching is not promised to any external society is plain; 1. Because all the constituent members of no such society are thus divinely taught. The visible Church includes "all sorts of men," good and bad, ignorant and enlightened, heterodox and orthodox, believing and infidel. Of the members of that society, therefore, that is not true which the Scriptures declare to be true, with regard to the members of the Church. They are not all taught of God. 2. Within the pale of every external, and especially of every denominational Church, there is heresy, either secret or avowed. But the teaching of God, as has been shown, precludes the possibility of fundamental error. There may be great diversity of views on many points of doctrine, but as to everything necessary to salvation, all the members of the body of Christ must agree. It is, however, notorious and avowed, that in the Church of Scotland, of England, and of Rome, all forms of doctrine, from the purest scriptural faith down to the lowest skepticism, are to be found; therefore, no such society can be the Church to which this divine teaching is promised. 3. The teaching of God being perpetual, securing constancy in the acknowledgment of the truth, none but those who continue in the truth can belong to the Church to which that teaching is promised. This fidelity is an attribute of the invisible Church alone, and therefore the communion of saints is the body to which this promise is made.

The Promise of Divine Protection to the Church
A third promise is that of divine protection. By this promise the Church is secured from internal decay and from external destruction. Its enemies are numerous and powerful; they are ever on the watch, and most insidious in their attacks. Without the constant protection of her divine Sovereign, the Church would soon entirely perish. This promise is made to every individual member of the Church. They are all the members of his body, and his body, redeemed and sanctified, can never perish. No man, he says, shall

The Spiritual Nature of the Church

ever pluck them out of his hand.[30] They may be sorely tempted; they may be seduced into many errors, and even into sin; but Satan shall not triumph over them. They may be persecuted, and driven into the caverns and dens of the earth, but though cast down, they are never forsaken.

That this promise of protection is not made to the external Church is plain, 1. Because multitudes included within the pale of that Church are not the subjects of this divine protection. 2. The external Church has not been preserved from apostasy. Both before and since the advent of Christ, idolatry or false doctrine has been introduced and tolerated by the official organs of that Church. 3. A society dispersed is, for the time being, destroyed. Its organization being dissolved, it ceases to exist as a society. From such disorganization or dispersion, the visible Church has not been protected, and therefore it cannot be the body to which this promise of protection belongs.

The Promise of a Universal Spiritual Kingdom

We find in the Scriptures frequent assurances that the Church is to extend from sea to sea, from the rising to the setting of the sun; that all nations and people are to flow unto it. These promises the Jews referred to their theocracy. Jerusalem was to be the capital of the world; the King of Zion was to be the King of the whole earth, and all nations were to be subject to the Jews. Judaizing Christians interpret these same predictions as securing the universal prevalence of the theocratic Church, with its pope or prelates. In opposition to both, the Redeemer said: "My kingdom is not of this world."[31] His apostles also taught that the kingdom of God consists in righteousness, peace, and joy in the Holy Ghost.[32] The extension

---

[30] John 10:28.
[31] John 18:36.
[32] Romans 14:17.

of the Church, therefore, consists in the prevalence of love to God and man, of the worship and service of the Lord Jesus Christ. It matters not how the saints maybe associated; it is not their association, but their faith and love that makes them the Church, and as they multiply and spread, so does the Church extend. All the fond anticipations of the Jews, founded on a false interpretation of the divine promises, were dissipated by the advent of a Messiah whose kingdom is not of this world.

History is not less effectually refuting the ritual theory of the Church, by showing that piety, the worship and obedience of Christ, the true kingdom of God, is extending far beyond the limits which that theory would assign to the dominion of the Redeemer.

The great promise made to the Church is holiness and salvation. Christ, it is said, loved the Church, and gave himself for it, that he might sanctify and cleanse it with the washing of water by the word; that he might present it to himself a glorious Church, not having spot, or wrinkle, or any such thing; but that it should be holy and without blemish.[33] This and similar passages, plainly teach that holiness and salvation are promised to every member of the Church. This is obvious; 1. Because these are blessings of which individuals alone are susceptible. It is not a community or society, as such, that is redeemed, regenerated, sanctified, and saved. Persons, and not communities, are the subjects of these blessings. 2. This follows from the relation of the Church to Christ as his body. The members of the Church are members of Christ. They are in him, partakers of his life, and the subjects of his grace. 3. It is, in fact, a conceded point. It is the common doctrine of all Christians, that out of the Church there is no salvation, and within the Church there is no perdition. It is the doctrine of all ritualists that those

---

[33] Ephesians 5:25–27.

who die in communion with the Church are saved. To this conclusion they are unavoidably led by what the Scriptures teach concerning the Church, as the body of Christ, and temple of God. Protestants admit the justice of the conclusion. They acknowledge that the Bible as plainly teaches that every member of the Church shall be saved, as that every penitent believer shall be admitted into heaven. If this is so, as both parties virtually concede, it determines the nature of the Church. If all the members of the Church are saved, the Church must consist exclusively of saints, and not "of all sorts of men."

Membership in the Church being thus inseparably connected with salvation, to represent the Church as a visible society, is—1. To make the salvation of men to depend upon their external relation, entirely irrespective of their moral character. 2. It is to promise salvation to multitudes against whom God denounces wrath. 3. It is to denounce wrath on many to whom God promises salvation. 4. It therefore utterly destroys the nature of true religion.

The argument for the true doctrine concerning the Church, derived from the divine promises, is this. Those promises, according to the Scriptures, are made to the humble, the penitent and believing; the Church, therefore, must consist exclusively of the regenerated. Those to whom the promises of divine presence, guidance, protection, and salvation, are made, cannot be a promiscuous multitude of all sorts of men. That theory of the Church, therefore, which makes it an external society, is necessarily destructive of religion and morality. Of religion, because it teaches that our relation to God depends on outward circumstances, and not on the state of the heart and character of the life. If, by an external rite or outward profession, we are made "members of Christ," "the children of God," and "inheritors of the kingdom of heaven;" if we are thus united to that body to which all the promises are made; and if our connection with the Church or body of Christ, can be dissolved only by heresy, schism, or excommunication, then of necessity religion is mere formalism, Church membership is the only condition of salvation, and Church ceremonies the only exercises of piety.

The Destructive Views of Oxford and Rome

This natural tendency of the theory in question is, indeed, in many minds, counteracted by opposing influences. Men who have access to the Bible, cannot altogether resist the power of its truths. They are thus often saved, in a measure, from the perverting influence of their false views of the Church. The whole tendency, however, of such error, is to evil. It perverts one's views of the nature of religion, and of the conditions of salvation. It leads men to substitute for real piety the indulgence of religious sentiment. They expend on the Church as an aesthetic idea, or as represented in a cathedral, the awe, the reverence, the varied emotions, which simulate the fear of God and love of his excellence. This kind of religion often satisfies those whose consciences are too much enlightened, and whose tastes are too much refined, to allow them to make full use of the theory that the visible Church is the body of Christ, and all its members the children of God.

This doctrine is no less destructive of morality than of religion. How can it be otherwise, if all the promises of God are made to men, not as penitent and holy, but as members of an external society; and if membership in that society requires, as Bellarmine and Mr. Palmer, Oxford and Rome, teach, no internal virtue whatever? This injurious tendency of Ritualism is not a matter of logical inference merely. It is abundantly demonstrated by history. The ancient Jews believed that God had made a covenant which secured the salvation of all the natural descendants of Abraham, upon condition of their adherence to the external theocracy. They might be punished for their sins, but, according to their doctrine,

The Spiritual Nature of the Church

no circumcised Israelite ever entered hell. The effect of this doctrine was manifest in their whole spirit and character. External connection with the Church, and practice of its rites and ceremonies, constituted their religion. They would not eat with unwashed hands, nor pray unless towards Jerusalem; but they would devour widows' houses, and, for a pretense, make long prayers.[34] They were whited sepulchers, fair in the sight of men, but within full of dead men's bones and of all. uncleanness.[35] The same effect has been produced by the doctrine which makes salvation depend upon connection with a visible society, in the Greek and Latin Churches. Ecclesiastical services have taken the place of spiritual worship. Corruption of morals has gone hand in hand with the decline of religion. The wicked are allowed to retain their standing in the Church, and are led to consider themselves as perfectly safe so long as embraced within its communion; and no matter what their crimes, they are committed to the dust "in the sure hope of a blessed resurrection."

There is one effect of this false theory of the Church, which ought to be specially noticed. It is the parent of bigotry, religious pride combined with malignity. Those who cry, "The temple of the Lord, the temple of the Lord" are we, are an abomination in the sight of God.[36] That this spirit is the legitimate fruit of the ritual theory is plain. That theory leads a particular class of men to regard themselves, on the ground of their external relations, as the special favorites of heaven. It is of course admitted that a sense of God's favor, the assurance of his love, is the fountain of all holy affections and right actions. Hence the Bible is filled with the declarations of his love for his people; and hence the Holy Spirit is sent to shed abroad his love in their hearts. The assurance of the divine

---

[34] Luke 20:47.
[35] Matthew 23:27.
[36] Jeremiah 7:4.

favor, however, produces holiness, only when we have right apprehensions of God, and of the way in which his love comes to be exercised towards us. When we see that he is of purer eyes than to look upon sin; that it is only for Christ's sake he is propitious to the guilty; that the love and indulgence of sin are proof that we are not the objects of his favor, the more we see of our unworthiness, the more grateful are we for his undeserved love, and the more desirous to be conformed to his image. But when men believe they are the favorites of God, because members of a particular society, that no matter what their personal character, they are objects of God's special love, then the natural and inevitable effect is pride, contempt, intolerance, malignity, and, when they dare, persecution. The empirical proof of the truth of this remark is found in the history of the Jews, of the Brahmins, of the Mohammedans, and of the Christian Church. It is to be found in the practical effect of the doctrine in question, wherever it has prevailed. The Jews regarded themselves as the peculiar favorites of God in virtue of their descent from Abraham, and irrespective of their personal character. This belief rendered them proud, contemptuous, intolerant, and malignant towards all beyond their exclusive circle. In the Christian Church we always find the same spirit connected with this doctrine, expressed under one set of circumstances by anathemas, enforced by the rack and stake; under another, by denying the mercy of God to the penitent and believing, if not subject to "pastors having succession;" by setting up exclusive claims to be the Church of God; by contemptuous language and deportment towards their fellow Christians; and, as in the case of Mr. Palmer, with the open avowal of the right and duty of persecution.

Such are the legitimate effects of this theory; effects which it has never failed to produce. It is essentially Antinomian in its tendency, destructive of true religion, and injurious to holy living, and therefore cannot be in accordance with the word and will of God.

The Spiritual Nature of the Church

The only answer given to this fatal objection is an evasion. Ritualists abandon *pro hac vice* their theory.[37] They teach that to the visible Church, Christ has promised his constant presence, his guidance, his protection, and his saving grace; and that in order to membership in this Church, no internal virtue is required, no regeneration, piety, sanctity, visible or invisible. But when it is objected, that if the promises are made to the visible Church, they are made to the wicked, for the wicked are within the pale of that Church, they answer, "The wicked are not really in the Church;" the Church really consists of "the elect, the predestinated, the sanctified."[38] As soon, however, as this difficulty is out of sight, they return to their theory, and make the Church to consist "of all sorts of men." This temporary admission of the truth, does not counteract the tendency of the constant inculcation of the doctrine that membership in that body to which the promises are made, is secured by external profession. Wherever that doctrine is taught, there the very essence of Antinomianism is inculcated, and there the fruits of Antinomianism never fail to appear.

The Church's Spiritual Authority Belongs to its Spiritual Members

The same argument, afforded by a consideration of the promises made to the Church to determine its nature, flows from a consideration of its prerogatives. Those prerogatives are the authority to teach, and the right to exercise discipline. These are included in the power of the keys.[39] This is not the place for any formal exhibition of the nature and limitations of this power. To construct the argument to be now presented, it is only necessary to assume what all Christians concede. Christ has given his Church the authority

---

[37] *Pro hac vice* is a Latin phrase meaning "for this occasion."
[38] Palmer, *Treatise on the Church*, 1:139.
[39] See Matthew 16:19.

to teach, and to bind and loose. He has promised to ratify her decisions and to enforce her judgments. In this general statement all denominations of Christians agree. Our present question is, "To whom does this power belong?" To the Church, of course. But is it to the visible Church, as such, irrespective of the spiritual state of its members, or is it to the Church considered as the communion of saints? The answer to this question makes all the difference between Popery and Protestantism, between the Inquisition and the liberty wherewith Christ has made his people free.

Spiritual Prerogatives Belong to Those who Truly Have the Spirit
The prerogative in question does not belong to the visible Church, or to its superior officers, but to the company of believers and their appropriate organs, because it presupposes the presence and guidance of the Holy Spirit. It is only because the Church is the organ of the Spirit of Christ, and therefore only so far as it is his organ, that the teaching of the Church is the teaching of Christ, or that her decisions will be ratified in heaven. It has, however, been abundantly proved from the word of God, that the Holy Spirit dwells only in true believers; they only are his organs, and therefore it is only the teaching and discipline of his own people, as guided by his Spirit, that Christ has promised to ratify. To them alone belongs the prerogative in question, and to any external body, only on the assumption of their being, and only as far as they are what they profess to be, the true children of God. No external visible body, as such, is so far the organ of the Holy Spirit, that its teachings are the teaching of Christ, and its decisions his judgments. No such body is, therefore, the Church to which the power of doctrine, and the key of the kingdom of heaven have been committed.

The Spiritual Nature of the Church

*Christ Promises to Ratifies the Teachings
of Only those Guided by the Spirit*
As it is undeniable that the visible Church is always a mixed body, and often controlled in its action by wicked or worldly men, if Christ had promised to ratify the teaching and discipline of that body, he would be bound to sanction what was contrary to his own word and Spirit. It is certain that unrenewed men are governed by the spirit of the world, or by that spirit which works in the children of disobedience, and it is no less certain that the visible Church has often been composed, in great measure, of unrenewed men; if, therefore, to them has been committed this prerogative, then the people of God are, by Christ's own command, bound to obey the world and those governed by its spirit. If wicked men, whether in the Church or out of it, cast us out of their communion, because of the opposition between us and them, it is nothing more than the judgment of the world. It is neither the judgment of Christ, nor of his Church. But if true believers refuse us their fellowship, because of our opposition to them as believers, it is a very different matter. It is one thing to be rejected by the wicked because they are wicked, and quite another to be cast off by the good because they are good. It is only the judgment of his own people, and even of his own people, only as they submit to the guidance of his own Spirit, (i.e., of his people as his people) that Christ has promised to ratify in heaven. The condemnation of Christ himself by the Jewish Church, of Athanasius by the Church of the fifth century, of Protestants by the Church of Rome, was but the judgment of the world, and of him who is the god of this world.

*Christians Have a Duty to Test the Teaching
of Officers in the Visible Church*
If the power of the keys is, as ritualists teach, committed to the chief officers of the Church as a visible society, if it is their official prerogative, then there can be no such thing as the right of private

judgment. Such a right can have no place in the presence of the Spirit of God. If the chief officers of the Church, without regard to their character, are the organs of that Spirit, then all private Christians are bound to submit without hesitation to all their decisions. This, as is well known, is the doctrine and practice of all those churches which hold that the promises and prerogatives pertaining to the Church, belong to the Church as a visible society. All private judgment, all private responsibility, are done away. But according to the Scriptures, it is the duty of every Christian to try the spirits--whether they be of God, to reject an apostle, or an angel from heaven, should he deny the faith, and of that denial such Christian is of necessity the judge. Faith, moreover, is an act for which every man is personally responsible; his salvation depends upon his believing the truth. He must, therefore, have the right to believe God, let the chief officers of the Church teach what they may. The right of private judgment is, therefore, a divine right. It is incompatible with the ritual theory of the Church, but perfectly consistent with the Protestant doctrine that the Church is the communion of saints. The latter is consequently the true doctrine.

The Visible Church Has Often Been in Error
The fact that the teaching of the visible Church has so often been contradictory and heretical, that council is against council, one age against another age, one part of the Church against another part, is a clear proof that the prerogative of authoritative teaching was never given by Christ to any such erring body. And the fact that the external Church has so often excommunicated and persecuted the true people of God, is proof positive that hers are not the decisions which are always ratified in heaven.

There are many difficult questions respecting the "power of the keys," which are not here alluded to. All that is now necessary, is to show that this is a prerogative which cannot belong to the visible Church as such. It can belong to her only so far as she is the organ

The Spiritual Nature of the Church

of the Church invisible, to which all the attributes, the promises and prerogatives of the true Church are to be referred. And no more wicked or more disastrous mistake has ever been made, than to transfer to the visible society of professors of the true religion, subject to bishops having succession, the promises and prerogatives of the body of Christ. It is to attribute to the world the attributes of the Church; to the kingdom of darkness the prerogatives of the kingdom of light. It is to ascribe to wickedness the character and blessedness of goodness. Every such historical Church has been the world baptized; all the men of a generation, or of a nation, are included in the pale of such a communion. If they are the Church, who are the world? If they are the kingdom of light, who constitute the kingdom of darkness? To teach that the promises and prerogatives of the Church belong to these visible societies, is to teach that they belong to the world, organized under a particular form and called by a new name.

Chapter 4
The Visibility of the Church[1]

Our view of the attributes of the Church is of necessity determined by our view of its nature. There is no dispute between Romanists and Protestants, as to whether the Church is visible, perpetual, one, holy, catholic, and apostolical. This is universally conceded. The only question is as to the sense in which these attributes can be predicated of it. If the Church is, in its essential nature and external organization, analogous to an earthly kingdom, then its visibility, perpetuity, and all its other attributes, must be such as can pertain to such an organization. When we affirm that an earthly kingdom is visible and perpetual, we mean that its organization as a kingdom is conspicuous, notorious, seen of all men, and unchanging. The kingdoms of Babylon, Egypt, and of Rome, have passed away. They are no longer visible or extant. The Papacy has a visible existence of the same kind, and Romanists affirm it is to continue while the world lasts. The kingdom of England is the body of men professing allegiance to its laws, and subject to its sovereign. The Church, according to Romanists, is the body of men professing the true religion, and subject to the Pope. Bellarmine, therefore, says: "The church is an assembly of men so visible and palpable as is the assembly of the Roman people, or the kingdom of France, or the Republic of Venice."[2] As these bodies are equally external organizations, the visibility of the one is analogous to that of the other.

---

[1] This chapter was originally published by Hodge as "Visibility of the Church," *The Biblical Repertory and Princeton Review* 25 (1853): 670–685.
[2] Robert Bellermine, *Disputationes, De Ecclesia Militante*, III, 2 (*Opera* [1857], 2:75). Hodge quotes Bellermine in the Latin: "*Ecclesia est coetus hominum ita visibilis et palpabilis, u test coetus Populi Romani, vel regnum Galliae aut respublica Venetorum.*"

The Visibility of the Spiritual Church on Earth

But if the Church is the *coetus sanctorum*, the company of believers; if it is the body of Christ, and if his body consists of those, and of those only, in whom he dwells by his Spirit, then the Church is visible only in the sense in which believers are visible. England stands out before the world as an earthly kingdom; the members of Christ's body in England are no less conspicuous. That believers are there, that the Church is there, is a fact which can no more be rationally disputed, than the existence of the monarchy. But it does not follow that because [it is] equally visible, they are equally external organizations, and [it does not follow] that to deny that the Church, in its idea, is an external society, is to deny that it is visible. Protestants teach that the true Church, as existing on earth, is always visible [for the following reasons]:

True Believers Have Visible Bodies
As it consists of men and women, in distinction from disembodied spirits or angels. Its members are not impalpable and unseen, as those ministering spirits who, unrevealed to our senses, continually minister to the heirs of salvation. "Surely," exclaims Bellarmine, "the Church does not consist of ghosts!" Certainly not: and the suggestion of such an objection betrays an entire misconception of the doctrine he was opposing. Protestants admit that the Church on earth consists of visible men and women, and not of invisible spirits.

The Good Deeds of True Believers Are Visible
The Church is visible, because its members manifest their faith by their works. The fact that they are the members of Christ's body becomes notorious. Goodness is an inward quality, and yet it is outwardly manifested, so that the good are known and recognized as such; not with absolute certainty in all cases, but with sufficient clearness to determine all questions of duty respecting them. So,

The Visibility of the Church

though faith is an inward principle, it so reveals itself in the confession of the truth, and in a holy life, that believers may be known as a tree is known by its fruit. In the general prevalence of Arianism, the true Church neither perished nor ceased to be visible. It continued to exist, and its existence was manifested in the confessors and martyrs of that age. "When," says Dr. Jackson, "the doctrine of antichrist was come to its full growth in the Council of Trent, although the whole body of Germany, besides Chemnitz and others, and although the whole visible Church of France, besides Calvin and some such, had subscribed unto that Council, yet the true Church had been visible in those worthies."[3] Wherever there are true believers, there is the true Church; and wherever such believers confess their faith, and illustrate it by a holy life, there the Church is visible.

The Spiritual Character of True Believers Makes Them Visible
The Church is visible, because believers are, by their "effectual calling," separated from the world. Though in it, they are not of it. They have different objects, are animated by a different spirit, and are distinguished by a different life. They are visible, as a pure river is often seen flowing unmingled through the turbid waters of a broader stream. When the Holy Spirit enters into the heart, renewing it after the image of God, uniting the soul to Christ as a living member of his body, the man becomes a new creature. All men take knowledge of him. They see that he is a Christian. He renounces the ways of the world, separates himself from all false religions, and becomes an open worshipper of Christ, a visible member of the Church, which is Christ's body. When the early Christians heard the words of eternal life, and received the gospel in

---

[3] Thomas Jackson, "Treatise on the Church." This quotation can be found in Thomas Jackson and Robert Sanderson, *Two Treatises on the Church* (London: J. Hatchard & Son, 1843), 70. Jackson was a Tractarian who served as the president of Corpus Christi College in Oxford.

faith, they at once renounced idolatry, withdrew from all corrupt associations, and manifested themselves as a new people, the followers of the Lord Jesus. They were visible members of his body. Even though there was but one such man in a city, still the fact that he was a Christian became notorious; and if a visible Christian, a visible member of the Church. The true Church is thus visible throughout the world, not as an organization, not as an external society, but as the living body of Christ; as a set of men distinguished from others as true Christians. They are the epistles of Jesus Christ, known and read of all men. This is a visibility which is real, and may be, and often has been, and will hereafter be, glorious. The Church, in this sense, is a city set on a hill. She is the light of the world. She is conspicuous in the beauty of holiness. This is not, indeed, the visibility of a hierarchy, gorgeous in apparel, pompous in ritual services—a kingdom which is of this world. But it is not the less real, and infinitely more glorious. How unfounded, then, is the objection that the Church, the body of Christ, is a chimera, a Platonic idea, unless it is, in its essential nature, a visible society, like the kingdom of England or Republic of Switzerland! Apart from any outward organization, and in the midst of all organizations, the true Church is now visible, and she has left a track of glory through all history, since the day of Pentecost, so that it can be traced and verified, in all ages and in all parts of the world.

True Believers Are Made Visible in the External Church
The true Church is visible in the external Church, just as the soul is visible in the body. That is, as by the means of the body we know that the soul is there, so by means of the external Church, we know where the true Church is. There are, doubtless, among Mohammedans, many insincere and skeptical professors of the religion of the false prophet. No one can tell who they are, or how many there may be. But the institutions of Mohammedanism, its laws, its usages, its mosques, its worship, make it as apparent as the light of

The Visibility of the Church

day, that sincere believers in Mahomet exist, and are the life of the external communities consisting of sincere and insincere followers of the prophet. So the external Church, as embracing all who profess the true religion—with their various organizations, their confessions of the truth, their temples, and their Christian worship—make it apparent that the true Church, the body of Christ, exists, and where it is. These are not the Church, any more than the body is the soul; but they are its manifestations, and its residence. This becomes intelligible by adverting to the origin of the Christian community. The admitted facts in reference to this subject are—1. That our Lord appeared on earth as the Son of God, and the Savior of sinners. To all who received him he gave power to become the sons of God: they were justified and made partakers of the Holy Ghost, and thereby united to Christ as living members of his body. They were thus distinguished inwardly and outwardly from all other men. 2. He commissioned his disciples to go into all the world and preach the gospel to every creature. He enjoined upon them to require as the conditions of any man's being admitted into their communion as a member of his body, repentance toward God, and faith in our Lord Jesus Christ. 3. He commanded all who did thus repent and believe, to unite together for his worship, for instruction, for the administration of the sacraments, and for mutual watch and care. For this purpose he provided for the appointment of certain officers, and gave, through his apostles, a body of laws for their government, and for the regulation of all things which those who believe were required to perform. Provision was thus made, by divine authority, for the Church assuming the form of an external visible society.

The Church as Visible and Invisible

The Church and the Lord's Supper

Let us now suppose that all those who, in every age, and in every part of the world, professed the true religion, and thereby united themselves to this society, were true believers, then there would be no room for the distinction, so far as this world is concerned, between the Church as visible and invisible. Then this external society would be Christ's body on earth. All that is predicated of the latter could be predicated of the former; all that is promised to the one would be promised to the other. Then this society would answer to the definition of the Church, as a company of believers. Then all within it would be saved, and all out of it would be lost. The above hypothesis, however, is undeniably false, and therefore the conclusions drawn from it must also be false. We know that even in the apostolic age, many who professed faith in Christ, and ranked themselves with his people, were not true believers. We know that in every subsequent age, the great majority of those who have been baptized in the name of Christ, and who call themselves Christians, and who are included in the external organization of his followers, are not true Christians. This external society, therefore, is not a company of believers; it is not the Church which is Christ's body; the attributes and promises of the Church do not belong to it. It is not that living temple built on the foundation of the apostles and prophets as a habitation of God, through the Spirit. It is not the bride of Christ, for which he died, and which he cleanses with the washing of regeneration. It is not the flock of the good Shepherd, composed of the sheep who hear his voice, and to whom it is his Father's good pleasure to give the kingdom. In short, the external society is not the Church. The two are not identical, commensurate, and conterminous, so that he who is a member of the one is a member of the other, and he who is excommunicated from the one is cut off from the other. Yet the Church is in that society, or the aggregate body of professing Christians, as the soul is in the body, or as sincere believers are comprehended in the mass of the professors of the religion of Christ.

The Visibility of the Church

If, then, the Church is the body of Christ; if a man becomes a member of that body by faith; if multitudes of those who profess in baptism the true religion, are not believers, then it is just as certain that the external body consisting of the baptized is not the Church, as that a man's calling himself a Christian does not make him a Christian. Yet there would be no nominal Christians, if there were no sincere disciples of Christ. The name and form of his religion would long since have perished from the world. The existence of the external Church, its continuance, its influence for good, its spiritual power, its extension, its visible organizations, are all due to the living element which it embraces, and which in these various ways manifests its presence. It is thus that the true Church is visible in the outward, though the one is no more the other than the body is the soul.

Proof from the Nature of the Church
That the Protestant doctrine as to the visibility of the Church, above stated, is true, is evident, in the first place, from what has already been established as to the nature of the Church. Everything depends upon the answer to the question, "What is the Church?" If it is an external society of professors of the true religion, then it is visible as an earthly kingdom; if that society is destroyed, the Church is destroyed, and everything that is true of the Church is true of that society. Then, in short, Romanism must be admitted as a logical necessity. But if the Church is a company of believers, then its visibility is that which belongs to believers; and nothing is true of the Church which is not true of believers.

Proof Found in Paul's Treatment of Israel
The Protestant distinction between the Church visible and invisible, nominal and real, is that which Paul makes between "Israel after the flesh," and "Israel after the Spirit." God had promised to

Israel that he would be their God, and that they should be his people; that he would never forsake or cast them off; that he would send his Son for their redemption; dwell in them by his Spirit; write his laws in their hearts; guide them into the knowledge of the truth; that he would give them the possession of the world, and the inheritance of heaven; that all who joined them should be saved, and all who forsook them should perish. The Jews claimed all these promises for the external organization, i.e., for the natural descendants of Abraham, united to him and to each other by the outward profession of the covenant, and by the sign of circumcision. They held, that external conformity to Judaism made a man a Jew, a member of that body to which all these promises and prerogatives belonged; and, consequently, that the apostasy or rejection of that external body would involve the destruction of the Church, and a failure of the promise of God. In like manner Ritualists teach that what is said and promised to the Church belongs to the external visible society of professing Christians, and that the destruction of that society would be the destruction of the Church.

In opposition to all this, Paul taught, 1. That he is not a Jew who is one outwardly. 2. Circumcision, which was outward, in the flesh, did not secure an interest in the divine promises. 3. That he only was a Jew, i.e., one of the true people of God, who was such in virtue of the state of his heart. 4. That the body to which the divine promises were made, was not the outward organization, but the inward, invisible body; not the Israel *kata sarka*,[4] but the Israel *kata pneuma*.[5] This is the Protestant doctrine of the Church, which teaches that he is not a Christian who is such by mere profession, and that it is not water baptism which makes a man a member of that body to which the promises are made, and consequently that

---

[4] Greek for "according to the flesh."
[5] Greek for "according to the Spirit."

The Visibility of the Church

the visibility of the Church is not that which belongs to an external society, but to true believers, or the communion of saints.

The perversion and abuse of terms, and the false reasoning to which Romanists resort, when speaking of this subject, are so palpable, that they could not be tolerated in any ordinary discussion. The word *Christian* is just as ambiguous as the word *Church*. If called upon to define a Christian, they would not hesitate to say: He is a man who believes the doctrines and obeys the commands of Christ. The inevitable inference from this definition is that the attributes, the promises, and prerogatives pertaining to Christians, belong to those only who believe and obey the Lord Jesus. Instead, however, of admitting this unavoidable conclusion, which would overthrow their whole system, they insist that all these attributes, promises, and prerogatives, belong to the body of professing Christians, and that it is baptism and subjection to a prelate or the pope, and not faith and obedience towards Christ, which constitute membership in the true Church.

Proof Taught in 1 John 2:19–20
The same doctrine taught by the apostle Paul, is no less plainly taught by the apostle John. In his day many who had been baptized, and received into the communion of the external society of Christians, were not true believers. How were they regarded by the apostle? Did their external profession make them members of the true Church, to which the promises pertain? St. John answers this question by saying, "They went out from us, but they were not of us; for if they had been of us, they would no doubt have continued with us: but they went out, that it might be made manifest that they were not all of us. But ye have an unction from the Holy One, and ye know all things."[6] It is here taught, 1. That many are included in the pale of the external Church, who are not members

---

[6] 1 John 2:19–20.

of the true Church. 2. That those only who have an unction of the Holy One, leading them into the knowledge of the truth, constitute the Church. 3. And consequently the visibility of the Church is that which belongs to the body of true believers.

Proof from When God's People Were Scattered
The Church must retain its essential attributes in every stage and state of its existence, in prosperity and in adversity. It is, however, undeniable, that the Church has existed in a state of dispersion. There have been periods when the whole external organization lapsed into idolatry or heresy. This was the case when there were but seven thousand in all Israel who had not bowed the knee to Baal, when at the time of the advent the whole Jewish Church, as an organized body, rejected Christ, and the New Testament Church was not yet founded; and to a great extent, also, during the ascendency of Arianism.[7] We must either admit that the Church perished during these periods, or that it was continued in the scattered, unorganized believers. If the latter, its visibility is not that of an external society, but such as belongs to the true body of Christ, whose members are known by the fruits of the Spirit manifested in their lives.

Proof from the Contrast between Scripture and Romanism
The great argument, however, on this subject, is the utter incongruity between what the Bible teaches concerning the Church, and the Romish doctrine that the Church is visible as an external organization. If that is so, then such organization is the Church; then, as the Church is holy, the body and bride of Christ, the temple and

---

[7] In parts of the fourth century, various forms of Arianism attracted many professing Christians, especially in periods where such views were supported by the Roman Emperor.

The Visibility of the Church

family of God, all the members of that organization are holy, members of Christ's body, and partakers of his life. Then, too, as Christ has promised to guide his Church into the knowledge of the truth, that external organization can never err as to any essential doctrine. Then, also, as we are commanded to obey the Church, if we refuse submission to this external body, we are to be regarded as heathen men and publicans. Then, moreover, as Christ saves all the members of his body and none other, he saves all included in this external organization, and consigns to eternal death all out of it. And then, finally, ministers admit to heaven all whom they receive into this society, and cast into hell all whom they reject from it. These are not only the logical, but the avowed and admitted conclusions of the principle in question. It becomes those who call themselves Protestants, to look these consequences in the face, before they join the Papists and Puseyites in ridiculing the idea of a Church composed exclusively of believers, and insist that the body to which the attributes and promises of the Church belong, is the visible organization of professing Christians.[8] Such Protestants may live to see men walking about with the keys of heaven at their girdle, armed with a power before which the bravest may well tremble.

Roman Catholic Objections to the Protestant View

The scriptural and Protestant doctrine of the visibility of the Church is, therefore, a corollary of the true doctrine of its nature. If the Church is a company of believers, its visibility is that which belongs to believers.[9] They are visible as men; as holy men; as men

---

[8] Edward Bouverie Pusey (1880-1882), a Church of England clergyman and professor of Hebrew at Oxford, was an important leader of the Oxford Movement—so much so that his name was turned into a label attached to those associated with it.

[9] Hodge is arguing here that the visibility of the church is not found in the visibility of its institution, organization, or hierarchical government. The visibility of the church is found in the visibility of its members—individual Christians who are the "soul" of external church organizations.

separated from the world, as a peculiar people, by the indwelling of the Spirit of God; as the soul and sustaining element of all those external organizations, consisting of professors of the true religion, united for the worship of Christ, the maintenance of the truth, and mutual watch and care.

Objection 1:
"The Church Is Spoken of in Scripture as a Visible Society"
The objections which Bellarmine, Bossuet, Palmer, and writers generally of the Romish and Ritual class, urge against this doctrine, are either founded on misconception, or resolve themselves into objections against the scriptural view of the nature of the Church as "the company of believers."[10] Thus, in the first place, it is objected that in the Scriptures and in all ecclesiastical history, the Church is spoken of and addressed as a visible society of professing Christians. The churches of Jerusalem, Antioch, Corinth, and Rome, were all such societies; and the whole body of such professors constituted the Church. History traces the origin, the extension, the trials, and the triumphs of that outward community. It is vain, therefore, to deny that body to be the Church, which the Bible and all Christendom unite in so designating. But was not the ancient Hebrew commonwealth called Israel, Jerusalem, Zion? Is not its history, as a visible society, recorded from Abraham to the destruction of Jerusalem? And yet does not Paul say expressly, that he is not a Jew who is one outwardly; that the external Israel is not the true Israel? In this objection the real point at issue is overlooked. The question is not, whether a man who professes to be a Christian, may properly be so addressed and so treated, but whether profession makes a mana true Christian. The question is

---

[10] Robert Bellarmine (1542-1621) was a leading Roman Catholic theologian who responded to Protestantism in the later part of the sixteenth century. Jacques Bossuet (1627–1704) was a Roman Catholic bishop in France and a leading theologian and political philosopher.

The Visibility of the Church

not, whether a society of professing Christians may properly be called a Church, and be so regarded, but whether their being such a society constitutes them a competent part of the body of Christ. The whole question is What is the subject of the attributes and prerogatives of the body of Christ? Is it the external body of professors, or the company of believers? If calling a man a Christian does not imply that he has the character and the inheritance of the disciples of Christ; if calling the Jewish commonwealth

Israel did not imply that they were the true Israel, then calling the professors of the true religion the Church, does not imply that they are the body of Christ. When the designation given to any man or body of men, involves nothing more than what is external or official, its application implies they are what they are called. To call a man an Englishman, is to recognize him as such. To address any one as emperor, king, or president, is to admit his claim to such title. But when the designation is expressive of some inward quality, and a state of mind, its application does not imply its actual possession, but simply that it is claimed. To call men saints, believers, the children of God, or a Church, supposes them to be true believers, or the true Church, only on the assumption that "no internal virtue" is necessary to union with the Church, or to make a man a believer and a child of God.

Scriptural and common usage, therefore, is perfectly consistent with the Protestant doctrine. That doctrine admits the propriety of calling any man a Christian who professes to be a worshipper of Christ, and of designating any company of such men a church. It only denies that he is a real Christian who is one only in name; or that that is a true Church, which is such only in profession. An external society, therefore, may properly be called a Church, without implying that the visibility of the true Church consists in outward organization.

The Church and the Lord's Supper

Objection 2:
"The Church Has All the Governing Structures of a Visible Society"

It is objected that the possession of officers, of laws, of terms of communion, necessarily supposes the Church to have the visibility of an external society. How can a man be received into the Church, or excommunicated from it, if the Church is not an outward organization? Did the fact that the Hebrews had officers and laws, a temple, a ritual, terms of admission and exclusion, make the external Israel the true Israel, or prove that the visibility of the latter was that of a state or commonwealth? Protestants admit that true believers form themselves into a visible society, with officers, laws, and terms of communion — but they deny that such society is the true Church, any further than it consists of true believers. Everything comes back to the question, "What is the Church?" True believers constitute the true Church; professed believers constitute the outward Church. These two things are not to be confounded. The external body is not, as such, the body of Christ. Neither are they to be separated as two churches; the one true and the other false, the one real and the other nominal. They differ as the sincere and insincere differ in any community, or as the Israel *kata pneuma*[11] differs from the Israel *kata sarka*.[12] A man could be admitted to the outward Israel without being received into the number of God's true people, and he could be excluded from the former without being cut off from the latter. The true Israel was not the commonwealth, as such, and the outward organization, with its laws and officers, though intimately related with the spiritual body as the true Church, did not constitute it. The question, how far the outward Church is the true Church, is easily answered. Just so far as it is what it professes to be, and no further. So far as

---

[11] Greek for "according to the Spirit."
[12] Greek for "according to the flesh."

The Visibility of the Church

it is a company of faithful men, animated and controlled by the Holy Spirit, it is a true Church, a constituent member of the body of Christ. If it be asked further, how we are to know whether a given society is to be regarded as a Church; we answer, precisely as we know whether a given individual is to be regarded as a Christian, i.e., by their profession and conduct. As the Protestant doctrine, that true believers constitute the body of Christ, is perfectly consistent with the existence among them and others outwardly united with them, of officers and laws, no argument can be drawn from the existence of such outward institutions to prove that the Church is essentially an external organization.

Bossuet presents this objection in the light of a contradiction. He says, "Protestants insist that the Church consists exclusively of believers, and is therefore an invisible body. But when asked for the signs of a Church, they say, the word and sacraments: thus making it an external society with ordinances, a ministry, and public service. If so, how can it consist exclusively of the pious? And where was there any such society, answering to the Protestant definition, before the Reformation?"[13] This objection rests upon the misconception which Ritualists do not appear able to rid themselves of. When Protestants say the Church is invisible, they only mean that an inward and consequently invisible state of mind is the condition of membership, and not that those who have this internal qualification are invisible, or that they cannot be so known as to enable us to discharge the duties which we owe them. When asked, "What makes a man a Christian?" we say, "true faith." When asked, "Whom must we regard and treat as Christians?" we answer, "Those who make a credible profession of their faith." Is there any contradiction in this? Is there any force in the objection, that if faith is an inward quality, it cannot be proved by outward evidence? Thus, when Protestants are asked, "What is the true

---

[13] Bossuet's *Variations*, Book xv, loc. 20.

Church?" they answer, "the company of believers." When asked, "What associations are to be regarded and treated as churches?" they answer, "those in which the gospel is preached." When asked further, "Where was the Church before the Reformation?" they answer, "just where it was in the days of Elijah, when it consisted of a few thousand scattered believers."[14]

Objection 3:
"How Could We Rightly Respond to the Church if it is Invisible?"
A third objection is very much of the same kind as the preceding. If the Church consists exclusively of believers, it is invisible. We are, however, required to obey the Church, to hear the Church, etc. But how can we hear and obey an invisible body? To this the answer is, the Church is no more invisible than believers are. We are commanded to love the brethren; to do good to all men, especially to the household of faith. As faith, however, is invisible, it may be asked, in the spirit of this objection, how can we tell who are believers? Christ says, by their fruits. There is no real difficulty in this matter. If we have a real heart for it, we shall be able to obey the command to love the brethren, though we cannot read the heart; and if disposed to hear the Church, we shall be able to recognize her voice. Because the true Church is always visible, and, therefore, can be obeyed, Ritualists infer that the visible Church is the true Church, though, as Dr. Jackson says, the two propositions differ as much as "to withstand a man" differs from "standing with a man."[15]

---

[14] Hodge adds in a footnote: "The question which Romanists so confidently ask, 'Where was your Church before Luther?' is well answered in the homely retort, 'Where was your face this morning before it was washing?'"

[15] This is a reference to the theologians Thomas Jackson (1579-1640). This reference can be found in Jackson's *A Treatise of the Holy Catholic Faith and Church*, book 12.

The Visibility of the Church

Objection 4:
"The People of God in the Old Testament Were a Visible Society"
Much the most plausible argument of Romanists is derived from the analogy of the old dispensation. That the Church is a visible society, consisting of the professors of the true religion, as distinguished from the body of time believers, known only to God, is plain, they say, because under the old dispensation it was such a society, embracing all the descendants of Abraham who professed the true religion, and received the sign of circumcision. To this external society were given the oracles of God, the covenants, the promises, the means of grace. Out of its pale there was no salvation. Union with it was the necessary condition of acceptance with God. This was a divine institution. It was a visible Church, consisting of professors, and not exclusively of believers. If such a society existed then by divine appointment, what has become of it? Has it ceased to exist? Has removing its restriction to one people destroyed its nature? Does lopping certain branches from the tree destroy the tree itself? Far from it. The Church exists as an external society now as it did then; what once belonged to the commonwealth of Israel, now belongs to the visible Church. As union with the commonwealth of Israel was necessary to salvation then, so union with the visible Church is necessary to salvation now. And as subjection to the priesthood, and especially to the high-priest, was necessary to union with Israel then, so submission to the regular ministry, and especially to the Pope, is necessary to union with the Church now. Such is the favorite argument of Romanists; and such, (striking out illogically the last clause, which requires subjection to prelates, or the Pope) we are sorry to say is the argument of some Protestants, and even of some Presbyterians.

How Should We Understand the Church's Relationship to Israel?

The fallacy of this whole argument [above] lies in the false assumption, that the external Israel was the true Church. It was not the body of Christ; it was not pervaded by his Spirit. Membership in it did not constitute membership in the body of Christ. The rejection or destruction of the external Israel was not the destruction of the Church. The apostasy of the former was not the apostasy of the latter. The attributes, promises, and prerogatives of the one, were not those of the other. In short, they were not the same, and, therefore, that the visibility of the one was that of an external organization, is no proof that the visibility of the Church is that of an external society. All this is included, not only in the express declaration of the Apostle, that the external Israel was not the true Israel, but is involved in his whole argument. It was, indeed, the main point of discussion between himself and the Jews. The great question was, is a man made a member of the true Israel, and a partaker of the promise, by circumcision and subjection, or by faith in Christ? If the former, then the Jews were right, and Paul was wrong as to the whole issue. But if the latter, then Paul was right and the Jews wrong. And this is the precise question between us and Romanists, and Anglicans [of the Oxford school]. If the external Israel was the true Israel, then Romanists are right and Protestants are wrong as to the method of salvation. Besides, if we admit that the external Israel was the true Church, then we must admit that the true Church apostatized; for it is undeniable that the whole external Israel, as an organized body, did repeatedly, and for long periods, lapse into idolatry. Nay more, we must admit that the true Church rejected and crucified Christ; for he was rejected by the external Israel, by the Sanhedrim, by the priesthood, by the elders, and by the people. All this is in direct opposition to the Scriptures, and would involve a breach of promise on the part of God. Paul avoids this fatal conclusion by denying that the external

The Visibility of the Church

Church is, as such, the true Church, or that the promises made to the latter were made to the former.

It is to be remembered that there were two covenants made with Abraham. By the one, his natural descendants through Isaac were constituted a commonwealth, an external, visible community. By the other, his spiritual descendants were constituted a Church. The parties to the former covenant were God and the nation; to the other, God and his true people. The promises of the national covenant were national blessings; the promises of the spiritual covenant, (i.e., of the covenant of grace,) were spiritual blessings, reconciliation, holiness, and eternal life. The conditions of the one covenant were circumcision and obedience to the law; the condition of the latter was, is, and ever has been, faith in the Messiah as the seed of the woman, the Son of God, and the Savior of the world. There cannot be a greater mistake than to confound the national covenant with the covenant of grace, and the commonwealth founded on the one with the Church founded on the other.

When Christ came, "the commonwealth" was abolished, and there was nothing put in its place. The Church remained. There was no external covenant, nor promises of external blessings, on condition of external rites and subjection. There was a spiritual society with spiritual promises, on the condition of faith in Christ. In no part of the New Testament is any other condition of membership in the Church prescribed than that contained in the answer of Philip to the eunuch who desired baptism: "If thou believest with all thine heart, thou mayest. And he answered and said, I believe that Jesus Christ is the Son of God" (Acts 8:37). The Church, therefore, is, in its essential nature, a company of believers, and not an external society, requiring merely external profession as the condition of membership. While this is true and vitally important, it is no less true that believers make themselves visible by the profession of the truth, by holiness of life, by separation from the world as a peculiar people, and by organizing themselves for the worship of Christ, and for mutual watch and care. The question, when any such organization is to be regarded as a portion of the true Church, is one to which the Protestant answer has already been given in a few words, but its fuller discussion must be reserved to some other occasion.

Chapter 5
The Perpetuity of the Church[1]

The Church is perpetual. Of this there is, among Christians, neither doubt nor dispute. But as to what is meant both by the subject and predicate of this proposition, there exist radically different views. By the Church, Romanists understand the external visible society united in the profession of the same faith, by communion in the sacraments, and subjection to bishops having succession, especially to the Roman Pontiff. The perpetuity of the Church, therefore, must on their theory include the continued existence of an organized society, professing the true faith; the continued legitimate administration of the sacraments; and the uninterrupted succession of prelates and popes.

Anglicans[2] understand by the Church an external society professing the true faith, united in the communion of the same sacraments, and in subjection to bishops canonically ordained. Perpetuity with them, therefore, must include perpetual adherence to the truth, the due administration of the sacraments, and the uninterrupted succession of bishops.

Protestants hold that the true Church is the body of true believers; and that the empirical or visible Church is the body of those who profess the true religion, together with their children.[3]

---

[1] This chapter was originally published by Hodge as "The Church—Its Perpetuity," *The Biblical Repertory and Princeton Review* 28 (1856): 689–715.

[2] Hodge: "By *Anglicans* is meant the Laudeans, or Oxford party, in the Church of England." Archbishop William Laud (1573-1645) was known for his strident advocacy of High Church formalism and ritualism. He was the Archbishop of Canterbury over the Church of England from 1633 to 1645.

[3] Hodge adds "together with their children," per the Westminster standards. Some Protestants (i.e. Baptists) do not view children as a part of the visible church, formally speaking.

All, therefore, that the perpetuity of the Church, according to the Protestant theory, involves, is the continued existence on earth of sincere believers who profess the true religion.

The Definition of the Church and Its Perpetuity

It is obvious that everything depends on the definition of the Church. If you determine the nature of the subject, you determine the nature of its attributes. If the Romish or Anglican definition of the Church be correct, then their view of all its attributes, its visibility, perpetuity, holiness, and unity, must also be correct. And, on the other hand, if the Protestant definition of the Church be accepted, so must also the Protestant view of its attributes. It is also obvious that the consideration of any one of these points involves all the others. The perpetuity of the Church, for example, brings up the question whether external organization is necessary to its existence; whether the Church may depart from the faith; whether the prelatical office is necessary, and whether an uninterrupted succession of ordination is essential to the ministry; how far the sacraments are necessary to the being of the Church; whether Peter was the head of the College of the Apostles; whether the bishop of Rome is his successor in that office; and whether submission to the Roman Pontiff is essential to the unity, and, of course, to the existence of the Church. All these points are involved in the Romish theory on this subject; and all, except the last two, in the Anglican doctrine. It would be impossible to go over all this ground in less compass than that of a volume. On each of these topics, ponderous tomes have been written. We propose simply to present, in a series of propositions, a brief outline of the Protestant answer to the question, "In what sense is the Church perpetual?"

The predictions of the Old Testament, and the promises of the New, it is universally conceded, secure the existence of the Church on earth until the second advent of Christ. Our Lord said to his disciples, "Lo, I am with you always, even to the end of the world."

The Perpetuity of the Church

He promised that the gates of hell should never prevail against his Church. As to the fact, therefore, that the Church is to exist on earth as long as the world lasts, there is and can be no dispute among Christians. The only question is, "How are these promises to be understood?"

Perpetuity Is Not Promised to Any Particular Body of Believers

The first proposition which Protestants maintain in answer to the above question, is, that the promise of Christ does not secure the continued existence of any particular Church as an organized body. By a particular Church is meant a body of professing Christians, united by some ecclesiastical organization, as the Church of Antioch, of Jerusalem, of England, or of Holland. The proposition is, that, from all that appears in Scripture, any such Church may apostatize from the truth, or cease to exist even nominally. This proposition is almost universally conceded. Many of the apostolic churches have long since perished. The Churches of Antioch, of Ephesus, of Corinth, of Thessalonica, have been blotted out of existence. Romanists teach that the Eastern Churches, and those of England, Scotland, Holland, etc., have so far departed from the faith and order of the true Church, as no longer to belong to the body of Christ. Anglicans teach, that all societies which have rejected the office, or lost the regular succession of the episcopate, have ceased to be Churches. Protestants, with one voice, deny that any particular Church is either infallible, or secure from fatal apostasy. All parties therefore agree in asserting that the promise of Christ does not secure the perpetuity of any one particular Church.

The great majority of Papists do indeed make an exception in favor of the city of Rome. As the bishop of that city is regarded as the vicar of Christ, and as all other Churches are required to recognize and obey him as such on pain of exclusion from the body of Christ, so long as the Church continues on earth, that bishop must continue worthy of recognition and obedience. Any member of the body may die, but if the head perish, the whole body perishes with it.

But since there is no special promise in Scripture to the Church of Rome, it can be made an exception to the general liability to defection only on the assumption, 1. That Peter was made the head of the whole Church. 2. That the recognition of him in that character is essential to membership in the body of Christ. 3. That he was the bishop of Rome. 4. That the popes are his legitimate successors in the bishopric of that city, and in his headship over the Church. 5. That the recognition of the supremacy of the Pope is an essential condition for all ages of the existence of the Church. Every one of these assumptions, however, is false.

The Church Exists Even in the Midst of Error

The second proposition is, that the promise of Christ does not secure his Church from all error in matters of faith. The Protestant doctrine is that a particular Church, and even the whole visible Church, may err in matters of doctrine, and yet retain their character as Churches. "The purest Churches under heaven," says the Westminster Confession, "are subject to mixture and error."[4] By the profession of the truth, therefore, which is declared to be essential to the existence of the Church, must be understood the profession of the fundamental doctrines of the gospel. This distinction between essential and non-essential doctrines is one, which however it may be denied, is in some form admitted by all Christians. Sometimes the distinction is expressed by drawing a line between matters of faith and matters of opinion; at others, by distinguishing between truths which must be received with explicit faith, and those which may be received implicitly. In some form the distinction must be acknowledged.

---

[4] Westminster Confession of Faith, XXV.5.

The Perpetuity of the Church

What we are concerned to show is that the existence of the Church does not depend on its absolute freedom from error. This may appear too plain a point to need proof; and yet it is one of the fundamental doctrines of Romanism, that the Church cannot err in matters of faith. That the Church may thus err is proved, 1. Because nothing can be necessary to the existence of the Church which is not necessary to salvation. Freedom from error in matters of doctrine, is not necessary to salvation, and therefore cannot be necessary to the perpetuity of the Church.

That nothing can be necessary to the existence of the Church which is not necessary to salvation, is so nearly a self-evident proposition, that its terms cannot be understood without forcing assent. Salvation involves union with Christ; union with Christ involves union with the Church, for the Church is his body; that is, it consists of those who are united to Him. Therefore, nothing which is compatible with union with Christ, can be incompatible with union to the Church. Consequently, the Church exists so long as true believers exist. It is a contradiction, therefore, to say that anything is necessary to the being of the Church, which is not necessary to salvation.

Individual Salvation Found in the midst of Error
That freedom from error in matters of faith is not necessary to salvation, is scarcely less plain. By "matters of faith" are meant those truths which God has revealed in his word, and which all who hear the gospel are bound to believe. Perfect faith supposes perfect knowledge; and such perfection cannot be necessary to salvation, because it is not necessary to piety. It is of course admitted that knowledge is essential to religion, because religion consists in the love, belief, and obedience of the truth. It is therefore conceded, that all religious error must be injurious to religion, in proportion to the importance of the truths concerned. If such errors are so grave as to present a false object of worship to the mind, or to lead

men to rest on a false ground of confidence, they must be fatal. But it must be admitted that a very limited amount of knowledge is absolutely essential to faith and love. A man may be ignorant of much that God has revealed, and yet receiving with humble confidence all he does know, and acting in obedience to what he has learned, he may be accepted of Him who judgeth according to that a man hath, and not according to that he hath not. As religion may consist with much ignorance, so it may consist with error. There is indeed little practical difference between the two. In both cases the proper object of faith and love is absent from the mind; and when absent its place is of necessity supplied by some erroneous conception. If a man know not the true God, he will form to himself a false god. If he know not that Jesus Christ is the Lord of glory, he will conceive him to be a man or angel. If he know not the true method of salvation, he will build his hope on some wrong foundation. But if perfect knowledge is not necessary to religion, freedom from error cannot be essential. And if not essential to the individual Christian, it cannot be essential to the Church, which is only a company of Christians. The Romish and Anglican doctrine, therefore, that all error in matters of faith is destructive to the being of the Church, or that the promise of Christ secures the Church from all such error, is contrary to the nature of religion, inasmuch as it supposes freedom from error to be necessary to its existence.

This view is confirmed by daily observation. We constantly see men who give every evidence of piety, who are either ignorant or erroneous as to many matters of faith. The Bible also, in various ways, teaches the same doctrine. It distinguishes between babes in Christ, and those who are strong. It recognizes as Christians those who know nothing beyond the first principles of the doctrines of Christ. It teaches that those who hold the foundation shall be saved (though so as by fire), although they build on that founda-

The Perpetuity of the Church

tion wood, hay, and stubble. It recognizes great diversity of doctrine as existing among those whom it treats as being substantially one in faith. It is not true, therefore, that a Christian cannot err in matters of faith; and if one may err, all may; and if all may, the Church may. The perpetuity of the Church consequently does not imply that it must always profess the truth, without any admixture of error.

The Church in Error throughout History
Secondly, the historical argument in opposition to the Romish doctrine that the Church must be free from error in matters of faith, is no less decisive.

There are two ways in which the Church may profess its faith. It may be done by its public authorized confession or creed; or it may be done by its individual members. The former is the more formal and authoritative; but the latter is no less real. The Church of any age consists of its members for that age. What the members profess, the Church professes. The apostasy of the Church of Geneva was not the less real, because the old orthodox Confessions were allowed to remain. The Churches of Germany were universally considered as sunk in Rationalism, even though the Augsburg Confession was nominally their standard of faith. The lapse of the Romish Church into infidelity and atheism in France was complete, although the Apostles' Creed continued to be professed in the Church services. If no Church could be considered as having lapsed into error, so long as its standards remain orthodox, then no Church can ever become erroneous, so long as it professes to believe the Scriptures. By the faith of a Church is properly meant the faith of its actual members; and by a Church professing error is meant that error is avowed by its members. The doctrine, therefore, that the Church cannot err in matters of faith, must mean that the mass of its members cannot thus err; for they constitute the Church, and if they err the Church errs.

There is no historical fact better established than that no external organized body has ever existed free from error. Even during the apostolical age the Churches of Jerusalem, of Corinth, and of Galatia, were infected with serious errors, and yet they were Churches. During the first three centuries, errors concerning the Trinity, the person and work of Christ, the person and office of the-Spirit, and the nature of man, were almost universal. From the fourth to the tenth century, no organized body can be pointed out whose members did not profess doctrines which are now almost universally pronounced to be erroneous. Since the Reformation, the Lutherans and the Reformed differ in matters of doctrine. The Church of England differs from the Greek and Latin Churches. So that it is impossible to maintain that freedom from error is essential to the perpetuity of the Church. No Church is absolutely pure in doctrine; and even if the standards of the Church should be faultless, still the real faith of its members is not. The promise of Christ, therefore, securing the perpetuity of the Church, does not secure the constant existence on earth of any body of men who are infallible in matters of faith and practice.

The Visibility of the Church is Not Essential to its Perpetuity

The third proposition is, that the perpetuity of the Church does not involve the continued existence of any visible organized body professing the true religion, and furnished with regular pastors.

At the time of the Reformation it was constantly urged against the Protestants that they were bound to obey the Church. To this they replied, that the Church to which the obedience of the faithful is due, was not the Romish, or any other external organization, for they had all departed from the faith, and taught for doctrines the commandments of men. To this, Romanists rejoined, that if that were true, the Church had perished, for no organized visible society could be pointed out which professed the doctrines avowed by

The Perpetuity of the Church

Protestants. To this again the Reformers replied, that the perpetuity of the Church, which all parties admitted, did not require the continued existence of any such society; the Church might exist, and at times had existed in scattered believers. Calvin says: "The hinges on which the controversy turns are these: first, in their contending that the form of the Church is always visible and apparent; and, secondly, in their placing this form in the see of the Church of Rome and its hierarchy. We, on the contrary, maintain, both that the Church may exist without any apparent form, and, moreover, that the form is not ascertained by that external splendor which they foolishly admire, but by a very different mark, namely, by the pure preaching of the word of God, and the due administration of the sacraments. They make an outcry whenever the Church cannot be pointed to with the finger."[5]

In support of what Calvin thus calls one of the cardinal doctrines of Protestants, that the Church may be perpetuated in scattered believers; or, in other words, that the apostasy of every visible organized society from the true faith is consistent with the perpetuity of the Church, it may be argued:

The Church as Defined by Protestants Is Perpetual
First, that the definition of the Church necessarily involves that conclusion. If the true Church consists of true believers, and the visible Church of professed believers, then the true Church continues as long as true believers exist on earth; and the visible Church so long as professors of the true religion exist. It is only by denying the correctness of these definitions that the necessity of a

---

[5] Hodge quotes Calvin in the Latin and adds this as a footnote: "Had Calvin lived in our day he would hear with surprise zealous Protestants, and even Presbyterians, crying out against the doctrine that visible organization is not essential to the Church." This block quotation of Calvin is taken from Calvin's Prefatory Address to Francis I in his Institutes. See John Calvin, *Institutes of the Christian Religion*, trans. Henry Beveridge (Grand Rapids: Hendrickson, 2008), xxi.

The Church and the Lord's Supper

continued visible organization can be maintained. Accordingly, Romanists and Anglicans have been obliged to depart from the scriptural view of the nature of the Church, and to make external organization an essential element of its definition in order to have any ground on which to stand. They maintain that the Church is something more than a company of believers, or a collective term for a number of believers. They insist that it is a visible organization, subject to lawful pastors — something that can be pointed to with the finger. If to such an organization the promise of perpetuity was originally given, then Protestants were schismatics, and their Churches are apostate. But if their view of the nature of the Church be correct, then their view of the sense in which it is perpetual must also be correct.

The Promise of Perpetuity Only Requires True Believers
Second, the promises of the word of God which secure the perpetuity of the Church, require nothing more than the continued existence of professors of the true religion. Thus, when our Lord says, the gates of hell shall never prevail against his Church; if by Church he meant his people, his promise only renders it certain that he shall always have a seed to serve him, or that there shall always be true followers and worshippers of Christ on the earth.[6] Thus, also, the declaration of Christ, "Lo, I am with you always, even unto the end of the world," holds good, even though all the temples of Christians should be destroyed, their faithful pastors scattered or slain, and they forced to wander about, being destitute, afflicted and tormented, hiding in dens and caves of the earth.[7] Nay, his presence will only be the more conspicuous in the sight of saints and angels, in sustaining the faith and patience of his people under all these trials, and in causing them to triumph

---

[6] Matthew 16:18.
[7] Matthew 28:20.

The Perpetuity of the Church

through suffering, and become great through weakness. The presence of God was more illustriously displayed with the three confessors in the fiery furnace, than with Solomon in all his glory. Protestants believe with Tertullian—"*Ubi tres sunt, etiamsi laici, ibi ecclesia est.*"[8]

The predictions in the Old Testament, which speak of an everlasting covenant which God was to form with his people, (Isaiah 61) and of a kingdom which shall never be destroyed (Dan. 2:44), do indeed clearly establish the perpetuity of the Church, but not of an external organization. The kingdom of God consists of those who obey him; and as long as there are any who recognize Christ as their king, so long will his kingdom continue. His promise renders it certain that such subjects of the heavenly King shall never entirely fail from among men; and also that their number shall ultimately so increase, that they shall possess the whole earth. More than this these predictions do not render [it] necessary. They do not preclude the possibility of the temporary triumph of the enemies of the Church, dispersing its members, and causing them to wander about, known only to God. Nor do they preclude the occurrence of a general apostasy, so extended as to embrace all the visible organizations calling themselves churches. Whether such an apostasy has ever actually occurred, is not now the question. All that is asserted is that these promises and predictions do not forbid its occurrence. They may all be yea and amen, though the faithful for a season be as few and as unknown, as the seven thousand who did not bow the knee unto Baal.[9]

Further, when St. Paul says, "Then we who are alive and remain, shall be caught up together with them in the air, and so shall

---

[8] Latin for "Where there are three, even if they are [only] laypeople, there the church is." See Tertullian, "On Exhortation to Chastity," Ch. 7.3.

[9] 2 Corinthians 1:20, 1 Kings 19:18.

The Church and the Lord's Supper

we be ever with the Lord" (1 Thessalonians 4:17), the only inference is that there shall be Christians living on the earth when Christ comes the second time. The parable of the wheat and tares proves that until the consummation there will be true and false professors of the religion of the gospel, but it proves nothing more.

Such are the leading scriptural arguments urged by Bellarmine[10] and Palmer[11] for the Romish and Anglican view of the perpetuity of the Church. They prove what Protestants admit, but they do not prove what their opponents assert. That is, they prove that the people of God shall continue to exist on the earth until the second coming of Christ, but they do not prove the continued existence of any visible organization professing the true faith, and subject to pastors having succession. If it be granted that the word *Church*, in Scripture, is a collective term for the people of God, then the promises which secure the continued existence of a seed to serve God as long as the world lasts, do not secure the continued fidelity of the visible Church, considered as an organized body.

The Unfolding of God's Redemptive Plan Doesn't Require a Visible Church

Third, another argument on this subject is, that there is no necessity for the continued existence of the Church as an external visible society. That is, there is no revealed purpose of God, which in-

---

[10] Hodge adds: *De Ecclesia*, cap. 12.

[11] Hodge adds: "Palmer on the Church, part i. ch. i. sec. 1. Mr. Palmer's chapter on this subject is one of the most illogical in all his elaborate work. Without defining his terms, he quotes promises and predictions which imply the perpetuity of the Church, and then quotes from Protestant writers of all denominations, passages to show that the continued existence of the Church is a conceded point. Every step of his argument, throughout his book, and all his important deductions, rest on the assumption that the Church, whose perpetuity is thus proved or conceded, is an external organization, consisting of those who profess the truth, without any error in matters of faith, and who are subject to pastors episcopally and canonically ordained. Everything is founded on this chapter, which quietly takes for granted the thing to be proved."

The Perpetuity of the Church

volves such existence as the necessary means of its accomplishment. Bellarmine's argument on this point is, "If the Church should ever be reduced to such a state as to be unknown, the salvation of those out of the Church would be impossible. For no man can be saved unless he enters the Church, but, if the Church be unknown, it cannot be entered, therefore, men cannot be saved."[12] Mr. Palmer's argument is to the same effect. "If the Church as an organization were to fail," he says, "there would be no way to revive it, except by a direct and immediate interposition of God; which would prove the gospel to be a temporary dispensation, and all living subsequently to its failure would be deprived of its benefits."

The answer to this is that the argument rests on the unscriptural assumption, that we become united to Christ by being united to the Church as an external visible society; whereas union with Christ in the divine order precedes, and is entirely independent of union with any visible society. "That our union with some present visible Church," says Dr. Jackson, one of the greatest divines of the Church of England, "is a native degree or part of our union with the Holy Catholic Church, [i. e., the body of Christ;] or, that our union with some present visible church is essential to our being, or not being members of the Holy Catholic Church," is what "we utterly deny."[13]

That such union with the visible Church as the argument of Bellarmine supposes, is not necessary to salvation is plain, because all that the Scriptures require in order to salvation, is repentance towards God, and faith in the Lord Jesus Christ. Baptism has indeed the necessity of precept, as something commanded; but even Romanists admit that where the desire for baptism exists, the mere

---

[12] Hodge adds "De Ecclesia, lib. iii. c. 13."
[13] Jackson and Sanderson, *Two Treatises on the Church*, x.

want of the rite works no forfeiture of salvation. And they also admit the validity of lay baptism; so that even if the necessity of that ordinance were conceded, it would not involve the necessity of an external organized Church, or an uninterrupted succession of the ministry. If, therefore, the whole visible organized Church should apostatize or be dispersed by persecution, the door of heaven would be as wide open as ever. Wherever Christ is known, men may obey and love him, without the intervention of a priest.

Mr. Palmer's idea, that if the Church as a society should fail, it could only be revived by a new revelation or intervention of God, rests on the assumption that the Church is a corporation with supernatural prerogatives and powers, which if once dissolved perishes entirely. The Church however is only the people of God; if they should be scattered even for years, as soon as they assemble for the worship of God, the administration of the Sacraments, and the exercise of discipline, the Church as a society is there, as good as ever; and a thousand times better than the fossil churches which have preserved their organic continuity only by being petrified. Should the succession of the ministry fail, no harm is done. The validity of the ministry does not depend on such succession. It is not the prerogative of prelates to make ministers. A minister is made by the inward call of the Spirit. The whole office of the Church in the matter is to sit in judgment on that call, and, if satisfied, to authenticate it. The failure of the succession, therefore, works no failure in the stream of life, as the Spirit is not confined to the channel of the ministry. The apostasy or dispersion of the whole organized Church, is not inconsistent with its continued existence, or incompatible with the accomplishment of all the revealed purposes of God. Men may still be saved, and the ministry and sacraments be perpetuated in all their efficiency and power.

Again, Bellarmine presents the following dilemma. "Either," he says, "those secret men who constitute the invisible Church, continue to profess the true religion or they do not. If they do, the

The Perpetuity of the Church

Church continues visible and conspicuously so, in them. If they do not confess the truth, then the Church in every sense fails, for without confession there is no salvation."

This is an illustration of the impossibility of errorists avoiding lapsing into the truth. Here is one of the acutest polemics Rome ever produced, surrendering the whole matter in debate. These secret confessors are not a society of faithful men, subject to lawful pastors and to the Pope. It is precisely what Romanists deny, and Protestants affirm, that the Church may be perpetuated in scattered believers, each in his own narrow sphere confessing the truth, and this is here conceded. This is what Protestants affirm of the Church before the Reformation. Every conspicuous organization had lapsed into idolatry, and yet the Church was continued in thousands of God's chosen ones who never bowed the knee to Baal.

God Tells of Times When the Visible Church Will Be Difficult To See

A fourth argument on this subject is derived from the predictions of general apostasy contained in the Scriptures. Our Lord foretold that false Christs should come and deceive many. He warned his disciples that they should be persecuted and hated of all nations; that iniquity should abound, and the love of many wax cold; that false prophets should arise and show signs and wonders, insomuch that, if it were possible, they would deceive the very elect. He intimated that faith should hardly be found when he came again; that it will be then as it was in the days of Noah, or in the time of Lot, only a few here and there would be found faithful. The apostles also are frequent and explicit in their declarations that a general apostasy was to occur. The Spirit, says Paul, speaketh expressly that in the latter times some shall depart from the faith (1 Timothy 4:1). In the last days, perilous times were to come (2 Timothy 3:4), times in which men would not endure sound doctrine,

(4:3). The day of Christ, he says, was not to come before the rise of the man of sin, whose coming was to be attended by the working of Satan, with all power, and signs, and lying wonders, when men (the professing Church generally) should be given up to believe a lie. Peter foretold that in the last times there should be false prophets and scorners, who would bring in damnable heresies (2 Peter 2:1, 3:3). And the apostle Jude reminds his readers of the words which were spoken by the apostles of the Lord Jesus Christ, how they told you that in the last time there should be mockers, walking after their own lusts (Jude 18).

Although these passages do not go the full length of the proposition above stated, or render it necessary to assume that no organized body was to exist during this apostasy, which professed the true faith, yet they are entirely inconsistent with the Romish and Anglican theory. That theory is that the catholic Church, or the great body of professing Christians united under lawful pastors, can never err in matters of faith. Whereas these passages foretell an apostasy from the truth so general, that true believers are to be few and scattered, driven into the wilderness, and in a great measure unknown to men.

The Old Testament Church Was Not Visible At Times
Fifth, the history of the Church before the advent of Christ, proves that its perpetuity does not involve the continued existence of any organization professing the true religion. The Church has existed from the beginning. We know, however, that there was, before the flood, an apostasy so general that Noah and his family were the only believers on the face of the earth. Soon after the flood the defection from the truth again became so far universal, that no organized body of the worshippers of God can be pointed out. Abraham was, therefore called to be the head of a new organization. His descendants, to whom pertained the law, the covenants, and the promises, constituted the visible Church; nevertheless,

The Perpetuity of the Church

they often and for long periods lapsed into idolatry. All public celebration of the worship of the true God was intermitted; altars to Baal were erected in every part of the land; the true children of God were scattered and unknown, so that under

Ahab, the prophet complained: "Lord, they have killed thy prophets, and digged down thine altars, and I am left alone." Where was then the visible Church? Where was then any organized society professing the true religion? The seven thousand who had not bowed the knee to Baal, were indeed the Church, but they were not an organized body. They were unknown even to Elijah.[14]

To this argument Bellarmine answers, that the Jewish Church was not catholic in the sense in which the Christian Church now is, because good men existed outside the pale of the Jewish Church: and therefore, although all within the Jewish communion had apostatized, it would not follow that the whole Church had failed. This is very true on the Protestant theory of the Church, but not on his. Protestants hold that the Church consists of true believers, and therefore so long as such believers exist, the Church exists. But according to Romanists the Church is a corporation, an external, visible, organized society. It is very clear that no such society existed except among the Jews, and therefore if the Jewish Church lapsed into idolatry, there was no Church on earth to answer to the Romish theory.

Another answer to the above argument is, that the complaint of Elijah had reference only to the kingdom of Israel; that although the defection there had been universal, the true Church as an organized body was continued in the kingdom of Judah. To this it may be replied, that the prophet probably intended to include both kingdoms, because he complains of digging down the altars of God; but there were no altars of God except at Jerusalem. Besides,

---

[14] See 1 Kings 19:10, 18.

the prophet could hardly have felt so entirely alone, and wished for death, if the worship of God were then celebrated at Jerusalem. What, however, is more to the purpose is, that it is plain that the apostle in Romans 11:2, evidently uses the word Israel not in its restricted sense for the ten tribes, but for the whole theocratical people. He appeals to the words of the prophet for the very purpose of proving that the rejection of the Jews as a body involved no failure of the divine promise. As in the days of Elijah there were an unknown few who, in the midst of general apostasy, did not bow to Baal; so notwithstanding the general defection and rejection of the Jews at the time of Christ, there was still a remnant according to the election of grace. Paul's design was to teach that the Church might be perpetuated, and in fact had been perpetuated in scattered unknown believers, although the visible Church as a society entirely apostatized.

Admitting, however, that the complaint of Elijah had exclusive reference to the kingdom of Israel, it still proves all that the argument demands. It proves that the Church as visible in that kingdom had apostatized and was continued in the seven thousand. This proves two points: first, that scattered believers, although members of no external society, may be members of the Church; and second, that the Church may be continued in such unknown believers. This is precisely what Romanists and Anglicans deny, and what Protestants affirm; and what Calvin declares to be one of the cardinal or turning points in our controversy with Rome.

Besides, whatever may have been the condition of the Church in Jerusalem at the period to which the prophet referred, it is certain that idolatry did at other times prevail contemporaneously in both kingdoms; and that after the captivity of the ten tribes, wicked kings set up idols even in the temple. Thus we read in 2 Chronicles 33:4-5 that Manasseh built altars in the house of the Lord, whereof the Lord had said, "In Jerusalem shall my name be forever. And he built altars in the two courts of the house of the

The Perpetuity of the Church

Lord… And he set up a carved image, the idol which he had made, in the house of God…made Judah and the inhabitants of Jerusalem to err and to do worse than the heathen." It is plain that the public worship of God, all the institutions of the Jewish Church, all sacrifices and service of the temple were abolished under this and other wicked princes. And when at last the patience of God was wearied out, Jerusalem itself was taken, the temple was destroyed, and the people carried away. During the seventy years of the captivity the visible Church as an organized body, with its priests and sacrifices, ceased to exist. It was continued only in the dispersed worshippers of the true God. Subsequently to the return of the people and the restoration of the temple, under the persecutions of Antiochus Epiphanes the public worship of God was again suppressed. Idols were erected in the temple, and altars dedicated to false gods were erected in every part of the land. It must be remembered that under the old dispensation the visible Church had, as it were, a local habitation. It was so connected with Jerusalem and the temple, that when those sacred places were in possession of idolaters, the Church was, for the time being, disorganized. No sacrifice could be offered, and all the functions of the priesthood were suspended.

There is another consideration which shows that the perpetuity of the Church does not depend on the regular succession of a visible society, and especially on the regular succession of the ministry, as Romanists and Anglicans assert. By the law of Moses, it was expressly ordered that the office of High Priest should be confined to the family of Aaron and descend in that family by regular descent. Even before the captivity, however, the priesthood was changed from one branch of that family to another, descending first in the line of Eleazar (Numbers 3:32, Deuteronomy 10:6) from Eli to Solomon in that of Ithamar; then returning to that of Eleazar (1 Samuel 2:35, 1 Kings 2:35). From the latter passage it appears that Solomon displaced Abiathar and appointed Zadok.

Under the Maccabees the office was given to the hero Jonathan, of the priestly family of Joiarib, (1 Maccabees 14:35, 41) after his death it was transferred to his brother Simon; and under Herod the office was sold to the highest bidder, or given at the discretion of the king (Josephus, *Antiquities*, xx.10). Caiaphas was made High Priest by Valerius Gratus, the Procurator of Judea, and soon after the death of Christ he was displaced by the Proconsul Vitellius (Josephus, 18.4, 3). If then, notwithstanding the express injunction of the law, the priesthood was thus changed, men being introduced into the office and displaced from it by the ruling powers without legitimate authority, and still the office continued, and the actual incumbent was recognized as high priest even by Christ and his apostles, it cannot be supposed that the existence of the Church is suspended on the regular succession of the ministry under the New Testament, where there is no express law prescribing the mode of descent. The Old Testament history, therefore, distinctly proves that the perpetuity of the Church involves neither the perpetual existence of an organized body professing the true religion, nor the regular transmission of the ministerial office. In other words, the apostolical succession in the Church or in the ministry, which is the great Diana of the Ephesians, is a mere figment.

Another illustration on this subject may be derived from the state of the Church during the time of Christ. The Jews were then divided into three sects, the Pharisees, the Sadducees, and the Essenes. Of these the Pharisees were the most correct in doctrine, and yet they made the word of God of no effect by their traditions, teaching for doctrines the commandments of men. They asserted the doctrine of justification by works in its grossest form; they attributed saving efficacy to external rites; and they were great persecutors of Christ. The people in their organized capacity, through their official organs, the priesthood and the Sanhedrim, rejected and crucified the Lord of glory. The Christian Church, as distin-

The Perpetuity of the Church

guished from the Jewish, was not organized until after the resurrection of our Lord. Where then, during the period referred to, was there any organized body which professed the true religion? The Protestant theory provides for this case, the Romish theory does not. The one theory is consistent with notorious historical facts; the other theory is inconsistent with them.

To all this, however, Bellarmine and others object that the privileges of the Christian Church are so much greater than those of the Jewish, that we cannot infer from the fact that the latter apostatized that the former may depart from the faith. To this we answer that the promises of God are the only foundation of the security of the Church. The promises addressed to the Jewish Church were as explicit and as comprehensive as those addressed to the Christian Church. If those promises were consistent with the apostasy of the whole organized body of the Jews, they must be consistent with a similar apostasy on the part of Christians. God promised to Abraham to be a God to him and to his seed after him; that though a woman might forsake her sucking child, he would never forsake Zion. But he did forsake Zion as an organized community; he did permit the seed of Abraham as a body to lapse into idolatry, to reject and crucify their Messiah; he permitted Jerusalem to be destroyed, and the people to whom were given the covenants, the law, and the promises, to be scattered to the ends of the earth. These promises, therefore, as Paul argues, were not intended to guarantee the continued existence of Israel as a society faithful to the truth, but simply the continued existence of true believers. As the Jews argued that the promises of God secured the continued fidelity of the external Israel; so Bellarmine and Mr. Palmer (Rome and Oxford) argue that his promises secure the continued fidelity of the visible Church. And as Paul teaches that the rejection of the external Israel was consistent with the fidelity of God, because the true Israel, hidden in the external body, continued faithful; so Protestants teach that the apostasy of the whole external organized Church is consistent with the promises of God, provided a remnant, however small and however scattered, adheres to the truth. The argument from the history of the Church under the old dispensation is therefore legitimate and scriptural. Nothing is promised to the Church now that was not promised to the Church then. Whatever happened to the one, may happen to the other.

The Church Was Not Visible at Times Throughout Church History
Sixth, the history of the Church since the advent of Christ is no less conclusive against the Romish theory. It is not necessary to assert that the whole visible church has at any time been so far apostate that no organized body existed professing the true faith. All that is requisite is to prove that the Church, in the sense in which Romanists and Anglicans understand the term, has at times denied the faith. By the Church they mean the multitude of professed Christians subject to Prelates or to the Pope. This body has apostatized. There have been times in which the Church has officially and by its appropriate and acknowledged organs (as understood by Ritualists) professed doctrines universally admitted to be heretical. Romanists and Anglicans say that this Church is represented by the chief pastors or bishops and that the decisions of these bishops, either assembled in council, or each acting for himself, are the decisions of the Church, to which all the faithful are bound to submit. The decision of the three hundred and eighty bishops assembled at Nicaea, in favor of the proper divinity of the Lord Jesus, is considered as the decision of the whole Church, notwithstanding the fewness of their number, and the fact that they were not delegates or representatives, and the further fact, that they were almost entirely from the West, because that decision was ratified by the silent acquiescence of the majority of the absent bishops. The fact that a great many of the Eastern bishops dissented from that decision and sided with Arius, is not allowed to

The Perpetuity of the Church

invalidate the authority of the council. By parity of reasoning, the decisions of the contemporaneous councils, that of Seleucia in the East, and of Ariminum in the West, were the decisions of the Church. Those councils together comprised eight hundred bishops; they were convened by the Emperor, their decisions were ratified by the Pope or bishop of Rome, and by the vast majority of the bishops of Christendom. Yet the decisions of these councils were heretical. They denied the proper Divinity of our Lord.

It cannot be pretended that the acquiescence in these decisions was less general than that accorded to those of the orthodox council of Nicaea. The reverse was notoriously the fact. Jerome in his dialogue "Contra Luciferianos" says: "The world was surprised to find itself Arian."[15] In his comment on Psalm 133, "The church is not held together by walls, but by the truth of its doctrines. Where the truth faith is, there is the church. Furthermore, after twenty or thirty years (Arian) heretics possessed all the walls of the church; however, the true church was there where true faith was."[16] Athanasius himself asks: "Now what church freely worships Christ? ...For if the pious and students of Christ are somewhere (and there are many tales everywhere) they also, like that great prophet Elijah, are hidden, and they hide themselves in caves and cracks of the earth or they remain wandering in solitary places."[17] Vincentius Lirinensis says: "Arian poison not only contaminated a little but almost the entire world, so almost all of the Latin sermons of

---

[15] Hodge quotes in Latin: "Ingemuit orbis terrarum, et se Arianum miratus est."

[16] Hodge quotes in Latin: "Ecclesia non in parietibus consistit, sed in dogmatum veritate; ecclesia ibi est, ubi fides vera est. Ceterum ante annos quindecim aut viginti parietes omnes ecclesiarum haeretici possidebant; ecclesia autem vera illic erat, ubi fides vera erat."

[17] Hodge quotes in Latin: "Quae nunc ecclesia libere Christum adorat? ...Nam si alicubi sunt pii et Christi studiosi (sunt autem ubique tales permulti) illi itidem, ut magnus ille propheta Elias, absconduntur, et in speluncas et cavernas terrae sese abstrudunt, aut in solitudine aberrantes commorantur (Lib. ad solitar. vitam agentes)."

the bishops spread a cloud of deceptive fog over all parts."[18] Thus according to Jerome the heretics were in possession of all church edifices; according to Athanasius the worshippers of Christ were hidden, or wandered about in solitude; and according to Vincent, the poison of Arianism infected the world. "After the defection of Liberius," says Dr. Jackson, "the whole Roman Empire was overspread with Arianism." If therefore the Church was orthodox under Constantine, it was heretical under Constantius. It professed Arianism under the latter, more generally than it had professed the truth under the former. For the bishops were "forty to one against Athanasius."

It will not avail to say that these bishops were deceived or intimidated. First, because the point is not why they apostatized, but that they did apostatize. This, the Romish and Anglican theory teaches, the representatives of the Church cannot do, without the Church perishing and the promise of God failing. And secondly, because the same objection might be made to the validity of the decisions of the council of Nicaea. Many bishops feigned agreement with those decisions; many signed them from fear of banishment; many because they thought they could be interpreted in a sense which suited their views. If these considerations do not invalidate the authority of the orthodox councils, they cannot be urged against the authority of those which were heterodox. Every argument which proves that the visible Church was Trinitarian at one time, proves that it was Arian at another time; and therefore the Church in the Romish and Anglican sense of that term, may apostatize.

---

[18] Hodge quotes in Latin: "Arianorum venenum non jam portiunculam quandam, sed pene orbem totum contaminaverat; adeo fere cunctis Latini sermonis episcopis partim vi partim fraude deceptis caligo qusedam offunderetur" (Adv. Haeres Novationes). The translation here is rough.

The Perpetuity of the Church

So undeniable is the fact of the general prevalence of Arianism, that Romanists and Anglicans are forced to abandon their fundamental principles, in their attempts to elude the argument from this source. Bellarmine says, the Church was conspicuous in that time of defection in Hilary, Athanasius, Vincent, and others.[19] And Mr. Palmer says the truth was preserved even under Arian bishops.[20] Here they are on Protestant ground. We teach that the Church is where the truth is; that the Church may be continued in scattered individuals. They teach that the Church, as an organized body, the great multitude of professors under prelates, must always profess the truth. The facts are against them, and therefore their doctrine must be false.

The Oxford Party Concedes that the True Church Was Perpetuated in Pre-Reformation Times
Seventh, the only other argument in favor of the position that the external Church may apostatize, is the concession of opponents. So far as the Anglican or Oxford party of the Church of England are concerned, they are estopped by the authority of their own Church and by the facts of her history.

Before the Reformation, that Church, in common with all the recognized Churches of the West, and the great body also of the Eastern Churches, held the doctrines of transubstantiation, the sacrifice of the mass, subjective justification, the priestly character of the ministry, the invocation of saints, the worship of images, extreme unction and purgatory. These doctrines the English Church rejected, pronouncing the mass idolatrous, and the other errors heretical. According to her own official declaration, therefore, the whole Church embraced in the Oxford definition of the term, had apostatized from the faith, and become idolatrous. To

---

[19] "De Ecclesia, lib. iii. cap. 16."
[20] "Palmer on the Church, vol. ii. p. 187."

The Church and the Lord's Supper

say, with the Anglican party, that the points of difference between Rome and England are matters of opinion, and not matters of faith, is absurd. Because both parties declare them to be matters of faith, and because they fall under the definition of matters of faith, as given by the Anglicans themselves. Any doctrine which the Church at any time has pronounced to be part of the revelation of God, they say is a matter of faith. But the doctrines above mentioned were all for centuries part of the faith of the whole catholic Church, and therefore cannot be referred to matters of opinion. It is, therefore, impossible that the Church of England can deny the proposition that the catholic Church, as a visible organization, may apostatize. All the great divines of England, consequently, teach that the Church may he perpetuated in scattered believers.

The concessions of Romanists on this point are not less decisive. They teach that when Antichrist shall come, all public worship of God shall be interdicted; all Christian temples shall be occupied by heretics and idolators, the faithful be dispersed and hidden from the sight of men in caves and dens of the earth. This is precisely what Protestants say happened before the Reformation. The pure worship of God was everywhere forbidden; idolatrous services were universally introduced; the true children of God persecuted and driven into the mountains or caves; false doctrine was everywhere professed, and the confession of the truth was everywhere interdicted.

Both parties agree as to what are the consequences of the coming of the man of sin. The only difference is that Protestants say he has come already,[21] and Romanists say his coming is still future. But if the promise of Christ that the gates of hell shall never prevail against his Church, consists with this general apostasy in the future, it may consist with it in the past. If the Church hereafter is to

---

[21] Many Protestants in Hodge's day believed that the "man of sin" (i.e., the antichrist) was the pope.

The Perpetuity of the Church

be hidden from view and continued in scattered believers, it may have been thus continued in times past. Romanists and Anglicans spurn with contempt the idea that the Lollards were the true Church in England, and yet they admit that when Antichrist shall come, the faithful will be reduced to the same, or even to a worse relative position. That is, they admit the external visible Church may become utterly apostate. Thus Bellarmine says: "It is certain that the persecution of the antichrist will be so severe and notorious that all public religious ceremonies and sacrifices will cease, and the Antichrist is going to forbid all the divine worship that is practiced in the Christian churches."[22] Stapleton says: "Of course the Church will be able to go into the wilderness during the reign of the Antichrist, and at that moment of time in the wilderness, that is in the secret places in the caves, in the hiding places where the saints receive themselves, the Church should not be uncomfortably sought."[23] During the reign of Antichrist, according to the notes to the Romish version of the New Testament (2 Thessalonians 2), "The external state of the Romish Church, and the public intercourse of the faithful with it, may cease; yet the due honour and obedience towards the Romish see, and the communion of heart with it, and the secret practice of that communion, and the open confession thereof, if the occasion require, shall not cease." Again, in verse 4, it is said: "The great Antichrist, who must come towards the world's end, shall abolish all other religions, true and false; and put down the blessed sacrament of the altar, wherein

---

[22] Hodge provides this reference: "Rom. Pontiff. lib. iii. c. 7." Hodge's quotation here is given by him in Latin: "Certum est, antichristi persecutionem fore gravissimam et notissimam ita ut cessant omnes publicae religionis ceremonise et sacrificia Antichristus interdicturus est omnem divinum cultum, qui in ecclesiis Christianorum exercetur."

[23] Hodge provides this reference: "Princip. Doctrin. cap. 2." Hodge's quotation here is also given in Latin: "Pelli sane poterit in desertum ecclesia, regnante Antichristo, et illo momento temporis in deserto, id est, in locis abditis, in speluncis, in latibulis quo sancti se recipient, non incommode quaereretur ecclesia."

consisteth principally the worship of the true God, and also all idols of the Gentiles." "The oblation of Christ's blood," it is said, "is to be abolished among all the nations and churches in the world."

These passages admit that as great an apostasy as Protestants have ever asserted has occurred. The public exercise and profession of the true faith is everywhere to cease: idolatry, or the worship of Antichrist, is to be set up in every church in the world; the only communion of the faithful is to be in the heart and in secret; believers are to be scattered and hidden from the sight of men. Romanists, therefore, although the admission is perfectly suicidal, are constrained to admit that the perpetuity of the Church does not involve the continuance of an external visible society, professing the true faith, and subject to lawful pastors. They give up, so far as the principle is concerned, all their objections to the Protestant doctrine, that the true Church was perpetuated during the Romish apostasy, in scattered believers and witnesses of the truth.

The Perpetuity of the Church Secure by the Continuance of True Believers

Eighth, the last proposition to be sustained, in vindicating the Protestant doctrine, is included in what has already been said. The Church is perpetual; but as its perpetuity does not secure the continued existence or fidelity of any particular Church; not the preservation of the Church catholic from all error in matters of faith; nor even the preservation of the whole visible Church as an organized body, from apostasy. The only sense in which the Church is necessarily perpetual, is in the continued existence of those who profess the true faith, or the essential doc- trines of the Scriptures.

The perpetuity of the Church in this sense is secured, 1. By the promises made to Christ, that he should see of the travail of his soul (Isaiah 53); that he should have a seed to serve him as long as

The Perpetuity of the Church

sun or moon endured (Psalm 72); that his kingdom was to be an everlasting kingdom, as foretold by all the prophets. 2. By the promises made by Christ, that the gates of hell should never prevail against his Church; that he would be with his people to the end of the world; that he would send them his Spirit to abide with them forever. 3. By the nature of the mediatorial office, Christ is the perpetual teacher, priest, and ruler of his people. He continues to exercise the functions of these several offices in behalf of his Church on earth; and therefore the Church cannot fail so long as Christ lives: "If I live," he says, "ye shall live also." 4. The testimony of history is no less decisive. It is true, it is not the province of history to preserve a record of the faith and knowledge of all the individuals of our race. The best men are often those of whom history makes no mention. And, therefore, though there were whole centuries during which we could point to no witnesses of the truth, it would be most unreasonable to infer that none such existed. The perpetuity of the Church is more a matter of faith, than a matter of sight; and yet the evidence is abundant that pious men, the children of God, and the worshippers of Christ, have existed in all ages of the world. There is not a period in the whole history of the world, and especially of the world since the advent of the Son of God, which does not in its literature retain the impress of devout minds. The hymns and prayers of the Church in themselves afford abundant evidence of its continued vitality. The history of the Church of Rome has been in great measure a history of the persecution of those who denied her errors, and protested against her authority; and therefore she has by the fires of martyrdom revealed the existence of the true Church, even in the darkest ages. The word of God has been read, even in the most apostate churches; the Psalter, the Creed, and the Ten Commandments, have always been included in the services of the most corrupt churches; so that in every age there has been a public profession of the truth, in which some sincere hearts have joined.

The Church and the Lord's Supper

This is not a point which needs to be proved, as all Christians are herein agreed. If, however, the Church is perpetual, it follows that everything necessary to its preservation and extension must also be perpetual. The Scriptures teach that the word, sacraments, and the ministry, are the divinely appointed means for that purpose; and on this ground we may be assured, prior to any testimony from history, that these means have never failed, and never shall fail. The word of God has never perished. The books written by Moses and the prophets are still in the hands of the Church. The writings of the apostles have been preserved in their integrity, and are now translated into all the important languages of the globe. It is impossible that they should perish. Their sound has gone into all the earth, and their words unto the ends of the world. So too with the sacraments. There is no pretense that baptism in the name of the Father, of the Son, and of the Holy Ghost has ever ceased to be administered agreeably to the divine command. And the Spirit of God has never failed to call men to the ministry of the word, and duly to authenticate their vocation. Whether there has been a regular succession of ordinations, is a small matter. Ordination confers neither grace nor office. It is the solemn recognition of the vocation of the Holy Ghost, which may be effectually demonstrated to the Church in other ways. The call of Farel and of Bunyan to the work of the ministry, though unordained by man (if such were the fact), is abundantly more evident than that of nine-tenths of the prelates of their day. In perpetuating his Church, God has therefore perpetuated his word, sacraments, and ministry, and we have his assurance that they shall continue to the end.

Concluding Argument

On the principles above stated, it is easy to answer the question so often put to Protestants by Romanists, "Where was your Church before the time of Luther?" Just where it was after Luther. "*Ubi vera*

The Perpetuity of the Church

fides erat, ibi ecclesia erat."[24] The visible Church among the Jews had sunk into idolatry before the time of Hezekiah. That pious king cast down the idols, and restored the pure worship of God. Did that destroy the Church? The Christian Church at Jerusalem was long burdened with Jewish rites. When they were cast aside, did the Church cease to exist? The Church in Germany and England had become corrupted by false doctrines, and by idolatrous and superstitious ceremonies. Did casting away these corruptions destroy the Church in those lands? Does a man cease to be a man, when he washes himself?

Or, if Bellarmine and Mr. Palmer may say that the Church was continued during the Arian apostasy in the scattered professors of the true faith, why may not Protestants say that it was continued in the same way during the Romish apostasy? If the Jewish Church existed when idolatry prevailed all over Judea, why may not the Christian Church have continued when image worship prevailed all over Europe? Truth alone is consistent with itself. The Protestant doctrine that the true Church consists of true believers, and the visible Church of professed believers, whether they be many or few, organized or dispersed, alone accords with the facts which Romanists and Protestants are alike forced to acknowledge. And that doctrine affords a ready answer to all objections derived from the absence of any conspicuous organization professing the true faith and worshipping God in accordance with his word. Admitting, therefore, that such witnesses of the truth as the Albigenses, Waldenses, and Bohemian brethren, do not form an unbroken succession of the visible Church, the doctrine that the Church is perpetual is none the less certain, and none the less consistent with Protestant principles. A man must be a Romanist in order to feel the force of the arguments of Romanists. He must believe the Church to be a visible society subject to the Pope, before he can be

---

[24] "Where true faith was, there was the church."

puzzled by the question, Where was the Church before the Reformation?

In like manner, if the above principles be correct, it is easy to see that the charge of schism cannot rest against Protestants. Schism is either separation, without just cause, from the true Church, or the refusing to commune with those who are really the children of God. If the Church consists of true believers, the Protestants did not withdraw from the fellowship of the Church; neither did they refuse to admit true believers to their communion. They did not form a new Church; they simply reformed the old. The same body which owned Jesus Christ as Lord, and professed his gospel from the beginning, continued to worship him and to confess his truth after the Reformation, without any solution in the continuity of its being. The fire which sweeps over the prairie may seem to destroy everything, but the verdure which soon clothes the fields with new life and beauty is the legitimate product of the life that preceded it. So the Church, although corruption or persecution may divest it of all visible indications of life, soon puts forth new flowers and produces new fruit, without any real discontinuance of its life. The only schismatics in the case are the Romanists, who denounce and excommunicate the Protestants because they profess the truth.

Chapter 6
The Reformed Protestant Doctrine of the Lord's Supper[1]

It is confessedly a very difficult matter to obtain clear views of what was the real doctrine of the Reformed church on the Lord's Supper, during the sixteenth century. This difficulty arises from various sources. The subject itself is mysterious. The Lord's Supper is by all Christians regarded as exhibiting and, in the case of believers, confirming their union with the Lord Jesus Christ. Whatever obscurity rests on that union, must in a measure rest on this sacrament. That union, however, is declared to be a great mystery. It has always, on that account, been called the mystical union. We are, therefore, demanding too much when we require all obscurity to be banished from this subject. If the union between Christ and his people were merely moral, arising from agreement and sympathy, there would be no mystery about it; and the Lord's Supper, as the symbol of that union, would be a perfectly intelligible ordinance. But the scriptures teach that our union with Christ is far more than this. It is a vital union, we are partakers of his life, for it is not we that live, but Christ that liveth in us. It is said to be analogous to

---

[1] This chapter was originally published by Hodge as "Doctrine of the Reformed Church on the Lord's Supper," *The Biblical Repertory and Princeton Review* 20 (1848): 227–278. This chapter contains most of the first half of this article, which was written as a review of John W. Nevin's *The Mystical Presence* (Philadelphia: J. B. Lippincott, 1846). Hodge's main point in this article is to argue that the Reformed tradition did not hold to the high sacramentalism that was being asserted by Nevin and the Mercersberg theologians. Instead, the Reformed tradition rejected the notion that the sacraments are the essential and indispensable way that God distributes the grace of Christ and the gift of salvation. According to Hodge, it is "the universally received doctrine of the Reformed Church, that we receive Christ as fully through the ministry of the word as in the Lord's Supper."

our union with Adam, to the union between the head and members of the same body, and between the vine and its branches. There are some points in reference to this subject, with regard to which almost all Christians are agreed. They agree that this union includes a federal or representative relation, arising from a divine constitution; and on the part of Christ, a participation of our nature. He that sanctified and they who are sanctified are all of one. On this account he calls them brethren. Inasmuch as the children are partakers of flesh and blood, he also himself likewise took part of the same (Hebrews 2:11-14). It is in virtue of his assumption of our nature that he stands to us in the intimate relation here spoken of. It is agreed, further, that this union include on our part a participation of the Spirit of Christ. It is the indwelling of the Holy Spirit, who is the Spirit of Christ, and dwells without measure in him as our head, who dwells also in his people, so that they become one body in Christ Jesus. They are one in relation to each other, and one in relation to him. As the human body is one by being animated and pervaded by one soul, so Christ and his people are one in virtue of the indwelling of one and the same Spirit, the Holy Ghost. It is further agreed that this union relates to the bodies as well as the souls of believers. Know you not, says the apostle, that your bodies are the members of Christ; know ye not that your body is the temple of the Holy Ghost, who dwelleth in you?[2] The Westminster Catechism, therefore, says of believers after death, that their bodies being still united to Christ, do rest in their graves until the resurrection. This union was always represented as a real union, not merely imaginary nor simply moral, nor arising from the mere reception of the benefits which Christ has procured. We receive Christ himself, and are in Christ, united to him by the indwelling of his Spirit and by a living faith. So far all the Reformed, at least, are agreed.

---

[2] 1 Corinthians 6:15, 19.

Reformed Protestant Doctrine of the Lord's Supper

Do the scriptures teach, besides all this, that we are partakers of the human nature, of the real flesh and blood of Christ? This question Romanists and Lutherans answer in the affirmative. They teach the actual reception and manducation[3] of the real body of Christ. This the whole Reformed church denied, in England, Belgium, and Germany, as well as in Switzerland. But as Christ speaks of eating his flesh and drinking his blood, and we are said to have communion in them, the question is in what way this is to be understood? All the Reformed answered, that by receiving the body and blood of Christ is meant receiving their virtue or efficacy. Some of them said it was their virtue as broken and shed, i.e., their sacrificial virtue; others said, it was a mysterious, supernatural efficacy flowing from the glorified body of Christ in heaven; and that this last idea, therefore, is to be taken into the account, in determining the nature of the union between Christ and his people. Apart, therefore, from the mysteriousness of the subject, the diversity of views among the Reformed themselves, is one reason of the difficulty in determining the real doctrine of the church, on this subject. In some of the confessions we have the one, and in some the other of these modes of representation, brought to view.

Another source of difficulty is found in the fact, that almost all the Reformed confessions were framed for the express purpose of compromise. One great object of Calvin's life was to prevent the schism between the two branches of the Protestant church. He and the other authors of these symbols, therefore, were constantly endeavoring to frame a statement of this doctrine, which all parties, Lutheran, Zwinglian, and Calvinistic, could adopt. Union was at that time a matter of the last importance, not only on religious and ecclesiastical grounds, but for reasons connected with their political well-being and safety. The question about the Lord's Supper, was the only one which kept the parties separate. Here Luther was

---

[3] Physical eating.

inflexible and most unreasonably violent. The Lutherans were at this time far more numerous and powerful than the Reformed. To conciliate Luther was, therefore, a constant object of desire and effort. Conference after conference was held for this purpose. The Reformed on all these occasions, and in all their confessions, went as far as possible to meet the views of the Lutherans. It is not wonderful therefore that their language, should at times, be hard to reconcile with what was in fact the real doctrine of the Reformed church. We find Bucer signing a formula which satisfied Luther,[4] and Beza signing another, which satisfied the Romish commissioners, at Poissy.[5] It is fair to infer from these historical circumstances, that while the Reformed held a doctrine which admitted of expression in the language adopted, it might be much more simply and intelligibly expressed in other terms. And we find in fact, that as soon as this pressure from without was removed, all ambiguity as to the Reformed doctrine as to the Lord's Supper ceased. No one pretends to misunderstand the language of Turretin and Pictet, the contemporaries or immediate successors of Beza.[6] This suggests a third source of difficulty on this subject, the ambiguity of the terms employed in these confessions. The words, presence, real, true, flesh and blood, substance, etc., are all employed, in many cases, out of their ordinary sense. We are said to receive the true body and blood, but nothing material; the substance, but not the essence: the natural body, but only by faith. It is not easy to unravel these conflicting statements and to determine what they really mean. Besides all this it is hard to tell where to look for the authoritative exhibition of the Reformed doctrine.

---

[4] Hodge is likely thinking here of the Wittenberg Concord (1536), which the Reformed theologian Martin Bucer (1491-1551) helped compose.
[5] Hodge is referencing here the involvement of Theodore Beza (1519-1605) involvement with the Colloquy of Poissy, which took place in 1561.
[6] Francis Turretin (1623-1687) and Benedict Pictet (1655-1724) both followed Calvin and Beza as leading theologians in the city of Geneva.

Reformed Protestant Doctrine of the Lord's Supper

Shall we look to the private writings of the Reformers, or to the public confessions? If to the latter, shall we rely on those of Switzerland or on those of the Palatinate, France or Belgium? These, though they have a general coincidence, do not entirely agree. Some favor one interpretation, and some another. Dr. Nevin chooses to make Calvin the great authority, and pronounces the confessions of the Swiss churches "chaotic and contradictory." The most satisfactory method of proceeding, as we conceive, will be to quote in the first instance, those authorities which represent the Swiss views; secondly, those which present the views of Calvin; and thirdly, those symbols in which both parties concurred. Having done this, we propose to analyze these statements, and endeavour to determine their meaning.

The Zwinglian View

Ulrich Zwingli says: "The Lord's Supper is nothing else than the food of the soul, and Christ instituted the ordinance as a memorial of himself. When a man commits himself to the sufferings and redemption of Christ, he is saved. Of this he has left us a certain visible sign of his flesh and blood, both which he has commanded us to eat and drink in remembrance of him."[7] This is said in a document, presented to the council of Zurich in 1523. In his LXVII Articles published in 1523, he says, briefly on this subject, in article 17, "Christ who offered himself once upon the cross is the eternally sufficient offering and sacrifice for the sins of all believers. Whence it follows that the mass is not a sacrifice, but the commemoration of the sacrifice made upon the cross, and, as it were, a seal of the redemption effected by Christ." In the *Expositio Chr. Fidei*, written

---

[7] Hodge adds this note: "We use the name of Zwingli to characterize the form of doctrine which he actually taught, and which was adopted in the church of Zurich of which he was the pastor; not in the sense in which the term Zwinglian is popularly used, to designate what was really the Socinian or Remonstrant doctrine on the Sacraments."

just before his death and published by Bullinger, 1531, he says: "The natural substantial body of Christ in which he suffered, and in which he is now seated in heaven, at the right hand of God, is not in the Lord's supper eaten, corporeally, or as to its essence, but spiritually only. ... Spiritually to eat the body of Christ, is nothing else than with the spirit and mind to rely on the goodness and mercy of God through Christ. ... Sacramentally to eat his body, is, the sacrament being added, with the mind and spirit to feed upon him."[8] And afterwards, "We assert therefore that the body of Christ is not eaten in the supper in a gross carnal manner as the Papists pretend, but spiritually and sacramentally, with a devout, believing and holy mind, as St. Chrysostom says." In his *Epist. ad princip German* (Op. II. p. 546), he uses this language: "When the bread and wine, consecrated by the very words of Christ are distributed to the brethren, is not the whole Christ, as it were sensibly (if words are required, I will say more that I am wont to do) presented to the senses? But how? Is the natural body handled and eaten? By no means; but offered to the mind to be contemplated, for the senses we have the sacrament of this thing. ...We never have denied that Christ is sacramentally and *in mysterio* present in the Lord's Supper, as well on account of believing contemplation, as the whole symbolical service."[9]

The confessions which most nearly conform to this view are the *Confessio Tetrapolitana*, *The First Basel*, and *The First Helvetic Confession*. All these are apologetic. The last named protests against the representation that the Reformed regard the sacraments as mere badges of profession, asserting that they are also signs and means of grace. In Article 22, the Lord's Supper is called

---

[8] Hodge's note: "Nicmeyer Col. Conf. p. 44, 47." See Chapter 4 of Zwingli's *Short and Clear Exposition of the Christian Faith* in William John Hinke, *Ulrich Zwingli on Providence and Other Essays* (Eugene, OR: Wipf and Stock, 1999), 235–293.

[9] See Zwingli's *Letter to the Illustrious Princes of Germany* in Hinke, *Ulrich Zwingli*, 105–127.

Reformed Protestant Doctrine of the Lord's Supper

coena mystica,[10] "'in which *Christus* truly offers his body and blood, and hence himself, to his people; not as though the body and blood of Christ were naturally united with the bread and wine, or locally included in them, or sensibly there present, but in so far as the bread and wine are symbols, through which we have communion in his body and blood, not to the nourishment of the body, but of the spiritual or eternal life."

The most concise and perspicuous statement of this form of the doctrine is to be found in "The Sincere Confession of the ministers of the church of Zurich," dated 1545. Those ministers say: "We teach that the great design and end of the Lord's Supper, that to which the whole service is directed, is the remembrance of the body of Christ devoted, and of his blood shed for the remission of our sins. This remembrance however cannot take place without true faith. And although the things, of which the service is a memorial, are not visible or present after a corporal manner, nevertheless believing apprehension and the assurance of faith renders them present in one sense, to the soul of the believer. He has truly eaten the bread of Christ…who believes on Christ, very God and very man, crucified for us, on whom to believe is to eat, and to eat, to believe. … Believers have in the Lord's Supper no other lifegiving food than that which they receive elsewhere than in that ordinance. The believer therefore receives both, in and out of, the Lord's Supper in one and the same way; and by the same means of faith, one and the same food, Christ, except that in the supper the reception is connected with the actions and signs appointed by Christ, and accompanied with a testifying, thanksgiving and binding service…. Christ's flesh has done its work on earth having been offered for our salvation; now it no longer benefits on earth and is no longer here."[11] This is a remarkably clear and precise statement,

---

[10] Latin for "mystical supper."
[11] Hodge includes this note: "Gueriche: Symbolik. s. 452."

and should be remembered; for we shall find Calvin and others whose language is often so different, avowing their concurrence with these ministers of Zurich, or at least uniting with them in the statement of this doctrine.

Views of Calvin and of the Confessions Formed Under His Influence

John Calvin
John Calvin stated "We conclude that our souls are fed by the flesh and blood of Christ, just as our corporal life is preserved by bread and wine. For the analogy of the signs would not hold, if our souls did not find their aliment in Christ, which, however, cannot be the case, unless Christ truly coalesce into one with us, and support us through the use of his flesh and blood. It may seem incredible indeed that the flesh of Christ should reach us from such an immense local distance, so as to become our food. But we must remember how far the secret power of the Holy Spirit, transcends all our senses, and what folly it must be even to think of reducing his immensity to our measure. Let faith embrace then what the understanding cannot grasp, namely, that the Spirit unites things which are totally separated. Now this sacred communication of his flesh and blood, by which Christ transfuses his life into us, just as if he penetrated our bones and marrow, he testifies and seals in the holy supper; not by the exhibition of a vain and empty sign, but by putting forth such an energy of his Spirit as fulfils what he promises. What is thus attested he offers to all who approach the spiritual banquet. It is however fruitfully received by believers only, who accept such vast grace with inward gratitude and trust."[12]

---

[12] Calvin, *Institutes*, iv. 17, 10

Reformed Protestant Doctrine of the Lord's Supper

In 1561 Calvin wrote, in answer to the Lutheran Heshusius, and with a view to unite the two parties, his *Tract de vera participatione carnis et sanguinis Christi in sacra coena*.[13] In an appendix to that Tract, he says: "The same body then which the Son of God once offered in sacrifice to the Father, he daily offers to us in the supper, that it may be our spiritual aliment. Only that must be held which was intimated as to the mode, that it is not necessary that the essence of the flesh should descend from heaven, in order that we may feed upon it; but that the power of the Spirit is sufficient to penetrate through all impediments and to surmount all local distance. At the same time we do not deny that the mode here is incomprehensible to human thought; for flesh naturally could neither he the life of the soul, nor exert its power upon us from heaven; and not without reason is the communication, which makes us flesh of his flesh, and bone of his bones, denominated by Paul a great mystery. In the sacred supper we acknowledge it a miracle, transcending both nature and our own understanding, that Christ's life is made common to us with himself, and his flesh given us as aliment."

Again, "these things being disposed of, a doubt still appears with respect to the word substance; which is readily allayed, if we put away the gross imagination of a manducation of the flesh, as though it were like corporal food, that being put into the mouth, is received into the stomach. For if this absurdity be removed, there is no reason why we should deny that we are fed with Christ's flesh substantially, since we truly coalesce with him into one body by faith, and are thus made one with him. Whence it follows we are joined with him in substantial connection, just as substantial vigor flows down from the head into the members. The definition

---

[13] John Calvin, *True Partaking of the Flesh and Blood of Christ in the Holy Supper* in volume 2 of *John Calvin: Tracts and Letters*, ed. Henry Beveridge (Edinburgh: Banner of Truth, 2009), 496–572,

must then stand that we are made to partake of Christ's flesh substantially; not in the way of carnal mixture, or as if the flesh of Christ drawn down from heaven entered into us, or were swallowed by the mouth; but because the flesh of Christ, as to its power and efficacy, vivifies our souls, not otherwise than the body is nourished by the substance of bread wine."

We prefer giving these extreme passages as selected by Dr. Nevin instead of others of a different character, which could easily be gathered from Calvin's works. Those of the latter class, will turn up in their appropriate places. We proceed to quote some of the confessions, which most manifestly bear the impress of Calvin's hand or spirit.

The Gallican Confession

The Gallican Confession was adopted by the Protestants of France in 1559. In the 36th article it is said: "Although he be in heaven until he come to judge all the earth, still we believe that by the secret and incomprehensible power of his Spirit he feeds and strengthens us with the substance of his body and of his blood. We hold that this is done spiritually, not because we put imagination and fancy in the place of fact and truth, but because the greatness of this mystery exceeds the measure of our senses and the laws of nature. In short, because it is heavenly, it can only be apprehended by faith."[14] Article 37: "We believe, as has been said, that in the Lord's Supper, as well as in baptism, God gives us really and in fact

---

[14] Hodge quotes here the Latin text: "Quamvis (Christus) nunc sit in coelis, ibidem etiam remansurus donee veniat mundum judicaturus, credimus tamen, eum arcana et incomprehensibili Spiritus sui virtute nos nutire et vivificare sui corporis" and adds the following note: "Why Dr. Nevin, in his translation of this passage, should refer *apprehensa* to *virtute*, instead of *substantia*, we cannot tell." Hodge adds this Latin text to the Gallican confession, which is not found in most statements of the confession: "Dicimur autem hoc spiritualiter fieri, non ut efficacite et veritatis loco imaginationem aut cogitationem supponamus, sed potius, quoniam hoc mysterium nostrte cum Christo coalitionis tam sublime est, ut omnes nostros sensus totumque naturae ordinem superet, denique quoniam sit divinum ac coeleste, non nisi fide percipi at apprehendi potest."

that which he there sets forth to us; and that consequently with these signs is given the true possession and enjoyment of that which they present to us. And thus all who I bring a pure faith, like a vessel, to the sacred table of Christ, receive truly that of which it is a sign; for the body and the blood of Jesus Christ give food and drink to the soul, no less than bread and wine nourish the body."[15]

The National Synod of France
This is perhaps the proper place to state, though not in chronological order, that at a meeting of the National Synod of France, in 1571, Beza being president, an application was made by certain deputies to have the clause in Article 37 altered, which asserts that we are nourished with the "substance of Christ's body and blood." The synod refused to make the alteration and explained the expression by saying, they did not understand by it, "any confusion, commixture, or conjunction…but this only, that by his virtue, all that is in him that is needful for our salvation, is hereby most freely given and communicated to us. Nor do we consent with them who say we do communicate in his merits and gifts and spirit, without his being at all made ours; but with the apostle (Ephesians 5:23), admiring this supernatural, and to our reason incomprehensible mystery, we do believe we are partakers of his body delivered to death for us, and of his blood shed for us, so that we are flesh of his flesh, and bone of his bones, and that we receive him together with his gifts, by faith wrought in us by the incomprehensible virtue and efficacy of the Holy Spirit."[16] This decision was considered by the ministers of Zurich as involving a condemnation of their doctrine, and they complained of it accordingly. The following year, 1572, therefore the Synod decided, that though they chose to retain the word substance in the sense explained, they did so "without prejudicing those foreign churches, which for reasons best known to themselves do not use the word substance."

---

[15] Hodge's also quotes the Latin of Article 37.
[16] Hodge's note: "Quick's Synodicon, I. p. 92."

The Church and the Lord's Supper

And instead of saying as they had done the year before, "that we must truly participate in the second Adam, *that we may derive life from him;*" they substitute for the last clause the words: "that by mystical and spiritual communication with him, we may derive that true eternal life." "And the Lord's Supper," they add, "is principally instituted for the communication of it; though the same Lord Jesus be offered to us both in his substance and gifts, in the ministry of the word and baptism, and received by faith."[17]

The Synod of London

In the articles adopted by the Synod of London, in 1552, and sanctioned by the authority of Edward VI, the article on the Lord's Supper, gives in the first clause the scriptural language, "To those who receive it worthily and with faith, the bread which we break is the communion of the body of Christ," etc. The second clause rejects transubstantiation. The third denies the Lutheran doctrine, and asserts that as Christ is heaven: *any believer ought not to believe or declare that his body and blood, real and corporeal (as they may say) is present in the Eucharist.*[18]

The Thirty-Nine Articles

In the Thirty-Nine Articles of the Church of England, adopted in 1562, the article on the Lord's Supper corresponds in purport exactly in the first three clauses, with the article of Edward VI. Then follows these words: "The Body of the Lord is given, taken and eaten, in the Supper, only after a heavenly and spiritual manner. And the mean whereby the Body of Christ is received and eaten is

---

[17] Hodge's note: "Quick's Synodicon, I. p. 104."
[18] Hodge quotes the Latin here for the italics: "non debet quisquam fidelium carnis ejus et sanguinis realem et corporalem (ut loquantur) praesentiam in eucharistia vel credere vel profiteri."

Faith."[19] It is a remarkable fact that the Anglican confessions have decidedly a more Zwinglian tone than those of any other of the Reformed churches. This may in part be accounted for by the consideration that they were not irenical, drawn up to conciliate Lutherans.

The Scotch Confession

In the Scotch Confession of 1560 the language of Calvin is in a great measure retained. The only sentence that need be quoted is the following: "We confess that believers in the right use of the Lord's Supper thus eat the body and drink the blood of Jesus Christ, and we firmly believe that he dwells in them, and they in him, nay, that they thus become flesh of his flesh and bone of his bones. For as the eternal deity gives life and immortality to the flesh of Christ, so also his flesh and blood, when eaten and drunk by us, confer on us the same prerogatives."

The Belgic Confession

In the Belgic Confession adopted in 1563, the following words occur: "Christ hath not enjoined to us the use of his Sacraments in vain, so he works in us all that he represents to us by these holy signs, though the manner surpasses our understanding, and cannot be comprehended by us, as the operations of the Holy Ghost are hidden and incomprehensible. In the mean time we err not when we say that what is eaten and drunk by us is the proper and natural body and the proper blood of Christ. But the manner of our partaking of the same is not by the mouth, but by the Spirit

---

[19] Hodge quotes the Latin of Article XXVIII of the Lord's Supper here: "Corpus Christi datur, accipitur, et
    manducatur in coena, tantum coeleste et spirituali ratione. Medium autem quo corpus Christi accipitur et manducatur in coena fides est."

through faith" (Article 35).²⁰ It is not necessary to quote from other Confessions language of the same import with that already quoted. All the symbols above cited contain more or less distinctly the impress of Calvin's views, if we except perhaps those of the church of England, which as before remarked, are more of a Zwinglian cast.

Statements in which both Zwinglians and Calvinists Agreed

Consensus Tigurinus
Perhaps the most interesting and important document of this class is the *Consensus Tigurinus*. Switzerland had long been greatly distracted by the controversy on the sacraments. After much persuasion on the part of his friends, Calvin was induced to go to Zurich and hold a conference with Bullinger in 1549. The result of that conference was the adoption of the articles previously drawn up by Calvin himself, and afterwards published with the title: *Consentio mutua in re sacramentaria Ministrorum Tigurinae Ecclesiae, et D. Joannis Calvini Ministri Genevensis Ecclesiae, jam nunc ab ipsis authoribus edita*.²¹ We have, therefore, in this document the well-considered and solemnly announced agreement of the Zwinglian and Calvinistic portions of the Reformed church. This Consensus was soon made the object of vehement attack by the

---

[20] Hodge quotes the Latin here: "Christus testificatur, nos, quam vere hoc sacramentum manibus nostris accipimus et tenemus, illudque ore comedimus et bibimus, (unde et postmodum vita nostra sustentatur) tam vere etiam nos fide (quae animae et manus et os est) in animis nostris recipere verum corpus et verum sanguinem Christi, unici servatoris nostri ad vitam nostram spiritualem. Nequaquam erraverimus dicentes, id quod comeditur esse proprium et naturale corpus Christi, idque quod bibitur proprium esse sanguinem. At manducandi modus talis est, ut non fiat ore corporis, sed spiritu per fidem."

[21] John Calvin, *Mutual Consent in regard to the Sacraments between the Ministers of the Church of Zurich and John Calvin, Minister of the Church of Geneva, Now Published by Those who Framed it* in *Tracts and Letters*, II: 200-244.

Lutherans. Four years after its date, Calvin felt himself called upon to publish an explanation and defense of it. In his letter, prefixed to that defense, and addressed to the ministers of Zurich and other Swiss churches, he says: "The Lutherans now see that those whom they denounce as Sacramentarians agree, and then adds, "Even if the two excellent doctors, Zwingli and Oecolampadius, who were known to be faithful servants of Jesus Christ, were still alive, they would not change one word in our doctrine."[22]

This Consensus [Tigurinus] embraces twenty-six articles, all relating to the sacraments, and especially to the Lord's Supper. In these articles there is not a word, which any of the evangelical churches of the present day would desire to alter. We should like to print them all as the confession of our own faith on this whole subject. The first four are introductory. The fifth declares the necessity of our union with Christ, in order that we should partake of his life. The sixth declares that union to be spiritual, arising from the indwelling of the Spirit. The seventh sets forth the design of the sacraments. They are declared to be badges of profession and Christian communion, excitements to thanksgiving and to the exercise of faith, and to a holy life, and *syngraphae*[23] binding us thereto. Their principal end, however, is said to be that God therein may testify his grace to us, represent and seal it. For though they signify nothing not announced in the word, still it is a great thing, that they present, as it were, living images before our eyes, and which affect our senses and serve to lead us to the thing signified, while they recall to mind the death of Christ and all his

---

[22] Hodge quotes Calvin in the Latin here, and the passage referenced can be found in Calvin, *Tracts and Letters*, 2:211. Hodge also adds this note: "Compare with this the language of Dr. Nevin, who endeavors to represent the doctrine of Calvin and Zwingli on this subject to be as wide apart as the poles. He even says: 'If Calvinism, the system of Geneva, necessarily runs here into Zwinglianism, we may, indeed, well despair of the whole interest. For most assuredly no church can stand, that is found to be constitutionally unsacramental. p. 74.'"

[23] Latin for "signatures."

benefits, that our faith may be called into exercise; and besides this, what God had by his mouth declared, is here confirmed and sealed. The eighth declares that God inwardly works or communicates by his Spirit, the blessings signified by the sacraments. They are therefore, as stated in the ninth article, not naked signs, but as it is there expressed, "Though we distinguish, as is proper, between the sign and things signified, we do not disjoin the truth (or reality) from the signs; since all who by faith embrace the promises there presented, receive Christ with his spiritual gifts." In the tenth article, it is, therefore said, we should look at the promise rather than the signs. The signs without Christ, are declared in the eleventh article, to be *inanes larvae*.[24] The articles from the twelfth to the seventeenth, both included, relate to the efficacy of the sacraments. It is denied that they have any virtue in themselves, all their efficacy is referred to the attending power of God, which is exercised only in the elect, and therefore, it is added, the doctrine that the sacraments confer grace on all who do not oppose the obstacle of mortal sin, falls to the ground. In the eighteenth it is stated that the reason why the sacraments fail to benefit unbelievers is to be referred to their want of faith, and neither to the sacraments which always retain their integrity, nor to God. The nineteenth teaches that the blessings received in the sacraments, are by believers received on other occasions. And moreover, as is said in the twentieth, the benefit received from the sacraments, is not to be restricted to the time of administration, but may follow long afterwards. Those baptized in infancy are often regenerated in youth or even old age. In the twenty-first article all local presence of Christ in the Eucharist is denied. As a man he is in heaven, and is present only to the mind and faith. The twenty-second states that the words of institution, "This is my body," must be understood figuratively. In the twenty-third, it is taught that manducation of

---

[24] Latin for "empty ghosts."

Reformed Protestant Doctrine of the Lord's Supper

Christ's body implies no mixture or transfusion of substance, but the derivation of life from his body and blood as a sacrifice. The last three articles are directed against transubstantiation, the Lutheran doctrine of the local presence, and the adoration of the host.

The Heidelberg Catechism

The force of this document as an exhibition of the true doctrine of the Reformed church on this whole subject is greatly impaired in this meagre outline. We shall, however, have occasion to refer to its more explicit statements, in the progress of this investigation. The next witness to be cited is the *Heidelberg Catechism*. It was prepared at the command of Frederick III, elector of the Palatinate, by Caspar Olevian, a disciple of Calvin, and Ursinus, a friend of Melancthon, and adopted by a general synod held at Heidelberg in 1563. This catechism having symbolical authority, both in the German and Dutch Reformed churches, is entitled to peculiar respect as a witness to the faith of the Reformed church.

In answer to the 66th question the sacraments are declared to be "Sacred visible signs and seals, instituted by God, that through them he may more clearly present and seal the promise of the gospel, viz. that he, for the sake of the one offering of Christ accomplished on the cross, grants to us the forgiveness of sin and eternal life."[25]

In answer to the following question, it is stated, that the design both of the word and sacraments is to direct our faith to the sacrifice of Christ on the cross as the only ground of our faith.

Question 75: "How art thou reminded and assured, in the holy supper, that thou art a partaker of the one offering of Christ on the

---

[25] Hodge notes here that "There is some slight variation as to phraseology, between the German and Latin copies of this catechism. We unfortunately have not the authorized English version at hand, and therefore are obliged to translate, except where Dr. Nevin has given the English version, from the originals."

cross, and of all his benefits? Ans. Thus, that Christ has commanded me to eat of this broken bread, and to drink of this cup and has promised first, that as surely as I see with my eyes the bread of the Lord broken for me, and the cup handed to me, so surely was his body broken and offered for me on the cross, and his blood shed for me. Second, that he himself as certainly feeds and nourishes my soul to eternal life with his crucified body, and shed blood, as I receive from the hand of the minister, and after a corporal manner partake of the bread and wine, which are given as the svmbols of the body and blood of Christ."

Question 76: "What is it then to eat the crucified body and drink the shed blood of Christ? Ans. It is not only to embrace with a believing heart all the sufferings and death of Christ, and thereby to obtain the pardon of sin and eternal life; but also, besides that, to become more and more united to his sacred body, by the Holy Ghost who dwells both in Christ and in us; so that we, though Christ is in heaven and we on earth, are notwithstanding, flesh of his flesh and bone of his bones; and that we live and are governed forever by one Spirit, as the members of the same body are by one soul."

In the answer to the 78th, it is said that as in baptism the water is not changed into the blood of Christ, nor is itself the ablution of sin, but the symbol and pledge of those things, so in the Lord's Supper the bread is not the body of Christ, though from the nature of a sacrament and usage of scripture, it is so called.

In answer to Question 79, it is said the bread is called Christ's body, etc., "Not only thereby to teach us that as bread and wine support this temporal life, so his crucified body and shed blood are the true meat and drink whereby our souls are fed unto eternal life; but more especially, by these visible signs and pledges, to assure us, that we are as really partakers of his true body and blood (by the operation of the Holy Ghost), as we receive by the mouths of our bodies these holy signs in remembrance of him ; and that

Reformed Protestant Doctrine of the Lord's Supper

all his sufferings and obedience are as certainly ours as if we had in our own persons suffered and made satisfaction for our sins to God."

In the following question, "What is the difference between the Lord's Supper, and the Popish mass?" the first clause of the answer is: "The supper of the Lord testifies to us that we have perfect remission of all our sins, on account of the one sacrifice of Christ which he himself made once for all upon the cross; and also that we, by the Holy Spirit, are united to Christ, who according to his human nature is only in heaven at the right hand of the Father, and is there to be adored by us."

There is nothing in this account of the Lord's Supper to which exception would even now be taken. There is something in the answer to the 75th question, which seems evidently intended to cover Calvin's peculiar opinion of a miraculous influence from the body of Christ in heaven, but it is also as evidently intended to cover Bullinger's view on that subject. It is language to which Zwingli and Oecolampadius, as Calvin says on another occasion, would not object. This is the more remarkable when we consider the historical circumstances under which this catechism was drawn up, and its decidedly irenical object. No part of Germany was more distracted by the sacramentarian controversy than the Pilatinate. Nowhere was greater exertion made to conciliate the Lutherans by framing expressions which they could adopt. Yet this catechism, framed under these circumstances, teaches nothing to which the ministers of Zurich would be unwilling to subscribe.

The Second Helvetic Confession

The only other public symbol which it is necessary to cite, is the Second Helvetic Confession. This on some accounts is the most authoritative of all the confessions of the Reformed church.

It was drawn up by Bullinger in 1562. In 1565, the Elector Frederick, above mentioned, alarmed by the furious contentions in his dominions, and annoyed by the misrepresentations of the Lutherans, wrote to Bullinger to send him a confession which would if possible unite the parties, or at least silence the clamors of the Lutherans, and which the Elector might present at the approaching diet of the empire to refute the calumnies directed against the Reformed. Bullinger sent this confession which he had prepared some years before. The Elector was perfectly well-satisfied. To give it weight it was then sanctioned by the Helvetic churches, and soon became one of the most generally recognized standards of the Reformed in all parts of Europe. What it teaches on the Lord's Supper is entitled to be regarded as a fair exhibition of the real doctrine of the church. The fact that it was written by Bullinger, the successor of Zwingli at Zurich, the great opponent of what was considered peculiar in Calvin's views of this subject, would lead us to expect to find in it nothing but what the Zurich ministers could cordially adopt.

In the 19th chapter it is taught concerning the sacraments in general, 1. That they are mystic symbols, or holy rites, or sacred actions, including the word, signs, and the things signified. 2. That there were sacraments under the old as well as under the new economy. 3. That God is their author, and still operates through them. 4. That Christ is the great object presented in them, the substance and matter of them, the lamb slain from the foundation of the world, the rock of which all our fathers drank, &c. 5. Therefore as far as the substance is concerned, the sacraments of the two dispensations are equal; they have the same author, the same significancy and effect. 6. The old have been abolished, and baptism and the Lord's Supper introduced in their place. 7. Then follows an exposition of the constituent parts of a sacrament. First, the word, by which the elements are constituted sacred signs. Water, bread and wine, are, in themselves, apart from divine appointment, no sacred symbols. It is the word of God added to them, consecrating or setting them apart, which gives them their sacramental character.

Reformed Protestant Doctrine of the Lord's Supper

Secondly, the signs, being thus consecrated, receive the names of the things signified. Water is called regeneration, the bread and wine, the body and blood of Christ, i.e. the symbols or sacraments of his body and blood. They are not changed in their own nature. They are called by the names of the things signified, because the two are sacramentally united, that is, united by mystical significance and divine appointment. 8. In the next paragraph the confession rejects, on the one hand, the Romish doctrine of consecration; and, on the other, the opinion of those who either make the sacraments mere common signs, or entirely useless. 9. The benefits signified are not so included or bound to the sacraments, that all who receive the signs receive the things signified; nor does the efficacy depend on the administrator; nor their integrity, upon the receiver. As the word of God, continues his word, whether men believe or not, so it is with the sacraments.

The 21st chapter is devoted to the Lord's Supper. The following passages, which we prefer giving in the original,[26] will suffice to exhibit the doctrine here taught:

> But that it may the better and more plainly be understood how the flesh and blood of Christ are the meat and drink of the faithful, and are received by the faithful unto life eternal, we will add, moreover, these few things: Eating is of divers sorts. There is a corporeal eating, whereby meat is taken into a man's mouth, chewed with the teeth, swallowed down, and digested....

Nothing of this kind, of course is admitted with regard to the Lord's Supper.

---

[26] Hodge quotes the Latin from the twenty-first chapter of the Second Helvetic Confession in the next three paragraphs.

There is also a spiritual eating of Christ's body; not such a one whereby it may be thought that the very meat is changed into the spirit, but whereby (the Lord's body and blood remaining in their own essence and property) those things are spiritually communicated unto us, not after a corporeal, but after a spiritual manner, through the Holy Spirit, who does apply and bestow upon us those things (to wit, remission of sins, deliverance, and life eternal) which are prepared for us by the flesh and blood of our Lord, sacrificed for us; so that Christ does now live in us, as we live in him; and does cause us to apprehend him by true faith to this end, that he may become unto us such a spiritual meat and drink, that is to say, our life. ... And as we must by eating receive the meat into our bodies, to the end that it may work in us, and show its efficacy in us (because, while it is without us, it profiteth us not at all); even so it is necessary that we receive Christ by faith, that he may be made ours, and that he live in us, and we in him.... From all this it appears manifestly, that by spiritual meat we mean not any imaginary thing, but the very body of our Lord Jesus, given to us; which yet is received by the faithful not corporeally, but spiritually by faith... But this spiritual eating and drinking takes place also without the Supper of the Lord, even so often as, and wheresoever, a man does believe in Christ. To which purpose that sentence of St. Augustine does happily belong, "Why dost thou prepare thy teeth and belly? Believe, and thou hast eaten."

Besides that former spiritual eating, there is a sacramental eating of the body of the Lord; whereby the believer not only is partaker, spiritually and internally, of the true body and blood of the Lord, but also, by coming to the Table of the Lord, does outwardly receive the visible sacraments of the body and blood of the Lord.

We have thus furnished, as it appears to us, adequate materials for a clear and decided judgment as to what was the real doctrine of the Reformed church as to the Lord's Supper. We propose now to

Reformed Protestant Doctrine of the Lord's Supper

review these materials and apply them to the decision of the various questions agitated on this subject.

In what sense is Christ present in the Lord's Supper?

The authorities above cited, and the private writings of the Reformed theologians, are abundant in teaching that Christ is present in the Lord's Supper. They represent it as a calumny, when the Lutherans asserted that the Reformed regarded the bread and wine as representing the body and blood of Christ in no other sense than a statute represents Hercules or Mercury. Zwingli says, we have never denied that the body of Christ is sacramentally and mystically present in the Lord's Supper. They admitted not only that he is present as God and by his Spirit, but in an important sense as to his body and blood. The whole controversy relates to this latter point, viz., to the mode in which the body and blood of Christ are present in the Lord's Supper. In deciding this point, the Reformed theologians are very accurate in determining the different senses in which a thing may be said to be present. The word presence, they say, is a relative term, and cannot be understood without reference to the object said to be present, and the subject to which it is present. For presence is nothing but the application of an object to the faculty suited to the perception of it. Hence, there is a two-fold presence, viz., of things sensible and of things spiritual. The former are present, as the word imports, when they are *prae sensibus*,[27] so as to be perceived by the senses; the latter, when they are presented to the intelligence so as to be apprehended and enjoyed. Again, presence even as to sensible objects is not to be confounded with nearness. It stands opposed not to distance, but to absence. The sun is as near to us when absent at night, as when present by day. A thing therefore may be present as to efficacy and virtue, which is at a great distance locally. In which of

---

[27] Latin for "before the senses."

these senses are the body and blood of Christ present in the Lord's Supper? All the Reformed, in answer to this question, say that it is not in the sense of local nearness. The bread is neither transmuted into the body of Christ, as Romanists say, nor is his body locally present in, with and under the bread, according to the Lutheran doctrine. The presence is to the mind, the object is not presented to the senses, but apprehended by faith. It is a presence of virtue and efficacy not of propinquity.[28] All these statements, both negative and positive, are found in the authorities referred to in the preceding pages. The Helvetic Confession, chapter 21, says: "The body of Christ is in heaven at the right hand of God…. Yet the Lord is not absent from his church when celebrating his supper. The sun is absent from us in heaven, nevertheless it is efficaciously present with us: how much more is Christ, the Sun of righteousness, though absent as to the body, present with us, not corporally indeed, but spiritually, by his vivifying influence." Calvin, in the Consensus Tigurinus, Article 21, says: "Every imagination of local presence is to be entirely removed. For while the signs are here on earth seen by the eyes and handled by the hands, Christ, so far as he is a man, is nowhere else than in heaven; and is to be sought only by the mind and by faith. It is therefore an irrational and impious superstition to include him in the earthly elements." In the 10th article, it is taught that he is present in the promise, not in the signs.

Ursinus, the principal author of the Heidelberg Catechism, in his exposition of that formulary, says: "These two, the sign and the thing signified, are united together in this sacrament, not by any copulation, or corporal and local existence of one in the other, much less by transubstantiation, or changing the one into the other; but by signifying, sealing and exhibiting the one by the other. That is, by a sacramental union, whose bond is the promise

---

[28] Proximity.

Reformed Protestant Doctrine of the Lord's Supper

added to the bread, requiring the faith of the receivers. Whence it is clear, that these things in their lawful use, are always jointly exhibited and received, but not without faith of the promise, viewing and apprehending the thing promised, now present in the sacrament; yet not present or included in the sign as in a vessel containing it; but present in the promise, which is the better part, the life and soul of the sacrament. For they want judgment who affirm that Christ's body cannot be present in the sacrament, except it be in or under the bread; as if forsooth, the bread alone, without the promise, were either the sacrament, or the principal part of the sacrament."[29]

There is, therefore, a presence of Christ's body in the Lord's Supper; not local, but spiritual; not for the senses but for the mind and to faith; not of nearness but of efficacy. This presence (as Zwingli said, "if they want words"), the Reformed were willing to call real; if by real was understood not essential or corporal, but true and efficacious, as opposed to imaginary or ineffective. So far as this point is concerned there is no doubt as to the doctrine of the Reformed church.

What is meant by feeding on the body and blood of Christ?

This question does not relate to the thing received, but simply to the mode of receiving. What is intended by sacramental manducation?[30] In reference to this point, all the Reformed agreed as to the following particulars: 1. This eating was not with the mouth, either after the manner of ordinary food, which the Lutherans themselves denied, or in any other manner. The mouth was not, in this case, the organ of reception. 2. It is only by the soul that the body and blood of Christ are received. 3. It is by faith, which is declared to be the hand and the mouth of the soul. 4. It is by or

---

[29] Hodge notes: "Quoted by Dr. Nevin, p. 91."
[30] Eating.

through the power of the Holy Ghost. As to all these points there is a perfect agreement among the symbols of the Reformed church. Consensus Tigurinus, Article 23, says "That Christ feeds our souls with his body and blood, here set forth, by the power of the Holy Ghost, is not to be understood as involving any mixture or transfusion of substance, but that we derive life from his body once offered as a sacrifice, and from his blood shed as an expiation." The Belgic Confession, Article 35, says that God, it is said, sent Christ, as the true bread from heaven, "which nourishes and sustains the spiritual life of believers, if it be eaten; that is, if it be applied and received by the Spirit through faith." According to Ursinus, "There is then in the Lord's Supper a double meat and drink, one external, visible and terrene, namely, bread and wine; and another internal. There is also a double eating and receiving; an external and signifying, which is the corporal receiving of the bread and wine; that is, that which is performed by the hands, mouth and senses of the body; and an internal, invisible, and signified, which is the fruition of Christ's death, and a spiritual ingrafting into Christ's body; that is, which is not performed by the hands and mouth, but by the spirit and faith."

As to the question whether there is any difference between eating and believing, the authorities differ. The Zurich confession, and the Helvetic quoted above distinctly say there is not. The former says: "Eating is believing, and believing is eating." The latter says: "This eating takes place as often and whenever a man believes in Christ." So says the Belgic confession, just quoted. Calvin, however, makes a distinction between the two. Eating, he says, is not faith, but the effect of faith. "There are some," he says, "who define in a word, that to eat the flesh of Christ and to drink his blood, is no other than to believe on Christ himself. But I conceive that in that remarkable discourse, in which Christ recommends us to feed upon his body, he intended to teach us something more striking and sublime; namely, that we are quickened by a real participation of him, which he designates by the terms *eating* and *drinking*, that no person might suppose the life which we receive from him to consist in simple knowledge. ...At the same, we confess there is no eating but by faith, and it is impossible to imagine any other; but the difference between me and those whose opinion I now oppose, is this ... they consider eating to be faith itself, but I apprehend it to be rather a consequence of faith." We do not see the force of this distinction. It all depends upon the latitude given to the idea of faith. If you restrict it to knowledge and assent, there is room for the distinction between eating and believing. But if faith includes the real appropriation of Christ, it includes all Calvin seems to mean by both terms, eating and believing. This question is of no historical importance. It created no diversity of opinion, in the church.

The question, whether eating the flesh of Christ, and drinking his blood is confined to the Lord's supper; in other words, whether there is any special benefit or communion with Christ to be had there, and which cannot elsewhere be obtained, the Romanists and Lutherans answer in the affirmative; the Reformed unanimously in the negative. They make indeed a distinction between spiritual and sacramental manducation. What is elsewhere received by faith, without the signs and significant actions, is in the sacraments received in connection with them. This is clearly taught in the confession of Zurich, 1545, quoted above; also in the Second Helvetic Confession as has already been shown. That confession vindicates this doctrine from the charge of rendering the sacrament useless. For, as it says, though we receive Christ once, we need to receive him continually and to have our faith strengthened from day to day. Calvin teaches the same doctrine in the Consensus Tigurinus, Article 19: "The verity which is figured in the sacraments, believers receive *extra eorum usum*.[31] Thus in baptism, Paul's sins were

---

[31] Latin for "outside the use of them."

washed away, which had already been blotted out. Baptism was to Cornelius the laver of regeneration, though he had before received the Spirit. And so in the Lord's Supper, Christ communicates himself to us, though he had already imparted himself to us and dwells within us." The office of the sacraments, he [Calvin] teaches, is to confirm and increase our faith. In his defense of this Consensus, he expresses surprise that a doctrine so plainly proved by experience and scripture, should be called into question. (Niemeyer's Col. p. 212). In the decree of the French National Synod of 1572, already quoted, it is said, "The same Lord Jesus both as to his substance and gifts, is offered to us in baptism and the ministry of the word, and received by believers."

We find the same doctrine in the Book of Common Prayer of the Church of England. In the office for the communion of the sick, the minister is directed to instruct a parishioner who is prevented receiving the sacrament, "that if he do truly repent him of his sins, and steadfastly believe that Jesus Christ hath suffered death for him on the cross, and shed his blood for his redemption, earnestly remembering the benefits he hath thereby, and giving him hearty thanks therefor, he doth eat and drink the body and blood of our Saviour Christ profitably to his soul's health, though he do not receive the sacrament with his mouth." On this point there was no diversity of opinion in any part of the Reformed church. There was no communion of Christ, no participation of his body and blood, not offered to believers and received by them, elsewhere than at the Lord's table and by other means. This is exalting the grace of God without depreciating the value of the sacraments.

What is meant by the body and blood of Christ as received in the sacrament?

The language employed in answer to this question is very various. It is said, we received Christ and his benefits, his flesh and blood, his true body, his natural body, his substance, the substance of his flesh and blood. All these forms of expression occur. Calvin says, we receive the substance of Christ. The Gallican Confession says, "We are fed with the substance of his body and blood." The Belgic Confession says that we received "his natural body." The question is, what does this mean? There is one thing in which all parties agreed, viz., that our union with Christ was a real union, that we receive him and not his benefits merely: that he dwells in his people by his Spirit, whose presence is the presence of Christ. Though all meant this, this is not all that is intended by the expressions above cited. What is meant by saying we receive his flesh and blood, or the substance of them. The negative answer to this question given by the Reformers uniformly is that they do not mean that we partake of the material particles of Christ's body, nor do they express any mixture or transfusion of substance. The affirmative statement is, in general terms, just as uniform, that these expressions indicate the virtue, efficacy, life-giving power of his body.

But there are two ways in which this was understood. Some intended by it, not the virtue of Christ's body and blood as flesh and blood, but their virtue as a body broken and of blood as shed, that is, their sacrificial, atoning efficacy. Others, however, insisted that besides this there was a vivifying efficacy imparted to the body of Christ by its union with the divine nature, and that by the power of the Holy Ghost, the believer in the Lord's supper and elsewhere, received into his soul and by faith this mysterious and supernatural influence.

Christ's Body as the Purveyor of Divine Life
This was clearly Calvin's idea, though he often contented himself with the expression of the former of these views. His doctrine is fully expressed in the following passages. "We acknowledge, without any circumlocution that the flesh of Christ, is life-giving, not

only because once in it our salvation was obtained: but because now, we being united to him in sacred union, it breathes life into us. Or, to use fewer words, because being by the power of the Spirit engrafted into the body of Christ, we have a common life with him; for from the hidden fountain of divinity life is, in a wonderfully way, infused into the flesh of Christ, and thence flows out to us." Again: "Christ is absent from us as to the body, by his Spirit, however, dwelling in us, he so lifts us to himself in heaven, that he transfuses the life-giving vigor of his flesh into us, as we grow by the vital heat of the sun." From these and many similar passages, it is plain that Calvin meant by receiving the substance of Christ's body, receiving its virtue or vigor, not merely as a sacrifice, but also the power inherent in it from its union with the divine nature, and flowing from it as heat from the sun.

Christ's Body as the Procurer of Atonement

The other explanation of this matter is that by "receiving the substance of Christ's body," or by "receiving his flesh and blood," was intended "receiving their life-giving efficacy as a sacrifice once offered on the cross for us." This view is clearly expressed in the Zurich Confession in 1545: "To eat the bread of Christ is to believe on him as crucified. …His flesh once benefited us on earth, now it benefits here no longer, and is no longer here." The same view is expressed by Calvin himself in the Consensus Tigurinus in 1549. In the 19th article we are said to eat the flesh of Christ, "because we derive our life from that flesh once offered in sacrifice for us, and from his blood shed as an expiation." With equal clearness the same idea is presented in the Heidleberg Catechism in 1560. In question 79, it is his crucified body and shed blood which are declared to be the food of the soul. The same thing is still more plainly asserted in the Helvetic Confession in 1566, chapter 21. In the first paragraph, it is said, "Christ as delivered unto death for us

Reformed Protestant Doctrine of the Lord's Supper

and as a Savior is the sum of this sacrament." In the third paragraph this eating is explained as the application, by the Spirit, of the benefits of Christ's death. And lower down, the food of the soul is declared to be "the flesh of Christ delivered for us, and his blood shed for us."[32] Indeed as this confession was written by Bullinger, minister of Zurich, the great opponent of Calvin's peculiar view, it could not be expected to teach any other doctrine. In what is called the Anglican Confession, drawn up by Bishop Jewell 1562, the same view is presented. It is there said: "We maintain that Christ exhibits himself truly present... that in the supper we feed upon him by faith and in the spirit (*fide et spiritu*) and that we have eternal life from his cross and blood." To draw life from the cross is here the same as to draw it from his blood, and of course must refer to the sacrificial efficacy of his death.

Which View is the Reformed View?

The question now arises which of the two views above stated is entitled to be regarded as the real doctrine of the Reformed? The whole church united in saying believers receive the body and blood of Christ. They agreed in explaining this to mean that they received the virtue, efficacy or vigour of his body and blood. But some understood, thereby, the virtue of his body as broken and of his blood as shed, that is, their sacrificial efficacy. Others said that besides this, there was a mysterious virtue in the body of Christ due to its union with the divine nature, which virtue was by the Holy Spirit conveyed to the believer. Which of these views is truly symbolical? The fairest answer to this question probably is, neither to the exclusion of the other. Those who held to the one, expressed their fellowship with those who held the other. Calvin and Bullinger united in the Consensus Tigurinus from which the latter

---

[32] Hodge quotes the Second Helvetic Confession in Latin here: "caro Christi tradita pro nobis, et sanguis ejus effusus pro nobis" (chapter XXI).

view is excluded. Both views are expressed in the public confessions. Some have the one, some the other.

But if a decision must be made between them, the higher authority is certainly due to the doctrine of sacrificial efficacy first mentioned. 1. It has high symbolical authority in its favour, it being clearly expressed in the Consensus Tigurinus, the common platform of the church, on this whole subject, and in the Second Helvetic Confession, the most authoritative of all the symbols of the Reformed church, and even in the Heidleberg Catechism, outweighs the private authority of Calvin or the dubious expression of the Gallican, Belgic, and some minor Confessions. 2. What is perhaps of more real consequence, the sacrificial view, is the only one that harmonizes with the other doctrines of the church. The other is an uncongenial foreign element derived partly from the influence of previous modes of thought, partly from the dominant influence of the Lutherans and the desire of getting as near to them as possible, and partly, no doubt, from a too literal interpretation of certain passages of scripture, especially John 6:54-58 and Ephesians 5:30. It is difficult to reconcile the idea that a life-giving influence emanates from the glorified body of Christ, with the universally received doctrine of the Reformed Church, that we receive Christ as fully through the ministry of the word as in the Lord's Supper. However strongly some of the Reformed asserted that we partake of the true or natural body of Christ, and are fed by the substance of his flesh and blood, they all maintained that this was done whenever faith in him was exercised. Not to urge this point however. All the Reformed taught, Calvin perhaps more earnestly than most others, that our union with Christ since the incarnation is the same in nature as that enjoyed by the saints under the old dispensation. This is perfectly intelligible if the virtue of his flesh and blood, which we receive in the Lord's Supper, is its virtue as a sacrifice, because he was the Lamb slain from the foundation of the world. His sacrifice was as effectual for the salvation of Abraham as of Paul, and could be appropriated as fully by the faith of the one as by that of the other. But if the virtue in question is a mysterious power due to the hypostatical union, flowing from Christ's body in heaven, it must be a benefit peculiar to believers living since the incarnation. It is impossible that those living before the advent could partake of Christ's body, in this sense, because it did not then exist; it had not as yet been assumed into union with the divine nature. We find therefore that Romanists and nominal Protestants, make the greatest distinction as to the relation of the ancient saints to God and that of believers since the advent, between the sacraments of the one dispensation and those of the other. All this is consistent and necessary on their theory of the incarnation, of the church and of the sacraments, but it is all in the plainest contradiction to the doctrine of the Reformed Church.[33] Here then is an element which does not accord with the other doctrines of that church; and this incongruity is one good reason for not regarding it as a genuine portion of its faith.

Another good reason for this conclusion is, that the doctrine almost immediately died out of the church. It had no root in the system and could not live. We hear nothing from the immediate successors of Calvin and Beza, of this mysterious, or as it was sometimes called, miraculous influence of Christ's heavenly body. Turretin, Beza's contemporary, expressly discards it. So does Pictet, who followed Turretin, and so do the Reformed theologians as a body.[34] As a single indication of this fact we refer to Craig's catechism, written under an order of the General Assembly of the

---

[33] Hodge notes here: "If any one doubts this assertion, let him read Calvin's Institutes B. iv. c. 14. Sec. 20-25. This subject however will come up in another place."

[34] Hodge notes, "We had transcribed various authorities as to this point, but are obliged to exclude them for the want of space. We refer the reader only to Turretin's statement of the question as between the Reformed and Lutherans, where he will see this whole matter ventilated with that masterly discrimination for which Turretin is unrivalled. Theol. Elenct. III. p. 567."

Church of Scotland, of 1590, and sanctioned by that body in 1592.[35] It will be remembered that the Scotch confession of 1560, before quoted, follows the very language of Calvin on this particular point. In Craig's catechism however, we have the following exhibition of the subject. "Ques. What signifieth the action of the supper? Ans. That our souls are fed spiritually by the body and blood of Jesus Christ. John 6:54. Ques. 71. When is this done? A. When we feel the efficacy of his death in our conscience by the spirit of faith. John 6:33... Ques. 75. Is Christ's body in the elements? A. No, but it is in heaven. Acts 1:11. Ques. 76. Why then is the element called his body? A. Because it is a sure seal of his body given to our souls." In the "Confession of Faith used in the English congregation of Geneva," the very first in date of the symbols of the Scotch church, it is said: "So the supper declareth that God, a provident Father, doth not only feed our bodies, but also nourishes our souls with the graces and benefits of Jesus Christ, which the scriptures calleth eating of his flesh and drinking of his blood."[36]

It is of course admitted that a particular doctrine's dying out of the faith of a church, is, of itself, no sufficient evidence that it was not a genuine part of its original belief. This is too obvious to need remark. There is, however, a great difference between a doctrine's being lost by a process of decay and by the process of growth. It is very possible that a particular opinion may be engrafted into a system, without having any logical or vital union with it, and is the more certain to be ejected, the more vigorous the growth and healthful the life of that system. The fundamental principles of Protestantism are the exclusive normal authority of scripture, and justification by faith alone. If that system lives and grows it must throw off everything incompatible with those principles. It is the

---

[35] The author of this catechism was John Craig, a colleague of John Knox.
[36] This confession was originally published in 1556, with John Knox being a major contributor.

fact of this peculiar view of a mysterious influence of the glorified body of Christ, having ceased to live, taken in connection with its obvious incompatibility with other articles of the Reformed faith, that we urge as a collateral argument against its being a genuine portion of that system of doctrine. According to the most authoritative standards of the Reformed church, we receive the body and blood of Christ, as a sacrifice, just as Abraham and David received them, who ate of the same spiritual meat and drank of the same spiritual drink. The church is one, its life is one, its food is one, from Adam to the last of the redeemed.

What is the effect of receiving the body and blood of Christ?
This question is nearly allied to the preceding. In general terms it is answered by saying, that union with Christ, and the consequent reception of his benefits, is the effect of the believing reception of the Lord's Supper. In the Basel Confession, it is said, "So that we, as members of his body, as our true head, live in him and he in us." The Geneva Catechism says the effect is "That we coalesce with him in the same life." The Scotch Confession says, "We surely believe that he abides in them (believers) and they in him, so that they become flesh of his flesh and bone of his bones." The Heidelberg Catechism has much the same words, adding, "and ever live and are governed by one Spirit, as the members of our body by one soul." The Second Helvetic Confession says, the effect of the Lord's Supper is, such an application of the purchase of Christ's death, by the Holy Spirit, "that he lives in us and we in him." So the Anglican Confession and others.

In explaining the nature of this union between Christ and his people, the Reformed standards reject entirely, as we have already seen, everything like corporeal contact, or the mixture or transfusion of substance. The proof of this point has already been sufficiently presented. We add only the language of Calvin. He says in opposition to the Lutherans: "If they insist that the substance of

Christ's flesh is mingled with the soul of man, in how many absurdities do they involve themselves?"[37] See also his *Institutes*, iv, 17, 32. In this negative statement, as to the nature of this union, all the Reformed agreed. They agreed also in the affirmative statement that we receive Christ himself and not merely his benefits. The union with Christ is a real [union], and not an imaginary or merely moral one. This is often expressed by saying we receive the substance of Christ, i.e., as they explain it, Christ himself, or the Holy Spirit, by whom he dwells in his people.[38] Their common mode of representation is that contained in the Consensus Tigurinus: "This spiritual communion which we have with the Son of God, when he lives in us by his Spirit, makes every believer a partaker of all the blessings which reside in him."[39] The mode in which this subject is represented in scripture and in the Reformed standards, is, that when the Holy Spirit comes to one of God's chosen with saving power, the soul is regenerated; the first exercise of its new life is faith; Christ is thereby received; the union with him is thus consummated; and on this follows the imputation of righteousness and all saving benefits.

---

[37] Hodge adds: "See his Defence of the Consensus Tigurinus." This can be found in Calvin, *Tracts and Letters*, 2:245-345.

[38] Hodge notes: "All these forms of expressions, illustrated and interchanged as they are in the Confessions, occur also in the early Reformed theologians. Thus Turretin says: 'The union between Christ and us is never in scripture spoken of as bodily, but spiritual and mystical, which can only be by the Spirit and faith.' Tom. III. p. 676. 'The bond of our union…is on the part of Christ the efficacious operation of his Spirit, on our part, faith, and thence love.' p. 578. This union he adds, is called substantial and essential in reference to its verity. He asserts that we receive 'the substance of Christ.' 'Because Christ is inseparable from his benefits. The believers under the Old Testament are correctly said to have been made partakers of Christ himself, and so of his body and blood, which were present to their faith; hence they are said to have drunk of that rock, which was Christ.' p. 580."

[39] Hodge quotes the Latin here of the Consensus Tigurinus: "Haec spiritualis est communicatio quarn habemus cum filio Dei, dum Spiritu suo in nobis habitans faciat credentes omnes, omnium, quae in se resident, bonorum compotes."

Reformed Protestant Doctrine of the Lord's Supper

The only question is whether besides this union effected by the Holy Spirit, there is on our part any participation of Christ's human body or of his human nature as such. This takes us back to the question already considered, relating to the mode of reception and the thing received, when it is said in scripture, that we eat the flesh and drink the blood of the Son of Man. As to these questions, it will be remembered the Reformed agreed as to the following points: 1. That this reception is by the soul. 2. Through faith, not through the mouth. 3. By the power of the Holy Ghost. 4. That this receiving Christ's body is not confined to the Lord's Supper, but takes place whenever faith in him is exercised. 5. That it was common to believers before and after the coming of the Son of God in the flesh. We have here a complete estoppel of the claim of the authority of the Reformed church in behalf of the doctrine that our union with Christ involves a participation of his human body, nature, or life. If it be asked, however, in what sense that church teaches that we are flesh of Christ's flesh, and bone of his bones? The answer is, in the same sense in which Paul says the same thing. And his meaning is very plain. He tells us that a husband should love his wife as his own body. He that loveth his wife loveth himself. His wife is himself, for the Scriptures say, they are one flesh. All this he adds, is true of Christ and his people. He loves the church as himself. She is his bride; flesh of his flesh and bone of his bones. If the intimate relationship, the identification of feelings, affections and interests, between a man and his wife, if their spiritual union, justifies the assertion that that they are one flesh, far more may the same thing be said of the spiritual relation between Christ and his people, which is much more intimate, sublime and mysterious, arising, as it does from the inhabitation of one and the same Spirit, and producing not only a union of feeling and affection, but of life. The same apostle tells us that believers are one body and members one of another, not in virtue of their common human nature, nor because they all partake of the humanity of Christ, but because they all have one Spirit. Such as we understand it is the doctrine of the Reformed church and of the Bible as to the mystical union.

What efficacy belongs to the Lord's Supper as a sacrament?
On this point the Reformed, in the first place, reject the Romish doctrine that the sacraments contain the grace they signify, and that they convey that grace, by the mere administration, to all who do not oppose an obstacle. Secondly, the Lutheran doctrine, which attributes to the sacraments an inherent supernatural power, due indeed not to the signs, but the word of God connected with them, but which is nevertheless always operative, provided there be faith in the receiver. Thirdly, the doctrine of the Socinians and others, that the sacraments are mere badges of profession, or empty signs of Christ and his benefits. They are declared to be efficacious means of grace; but their efficacy, as such, is referred neither to any virtue in them nor in him that administers them, but solely to the attending operation or influence of the Holy Spirit, precisely as in the case of the Word. It is the *virtus Spiritus Sancti extrinsecus accedens*,[40] to which all their supernatural or saving efficacy is referred. They have, indeed, the moral objective power of significant emblems and seals of divine appointment, just as the Word has its inherent moral power; but their efficacy as means of grace, their power, in other words, to convey grace depends entirely, as in the case of the Word, on the co-operation of the Holy Ghost. Hence the power is in no way tied to the sacraments. It may be exerted without them. It does not always attend them, nor is it confined to the time, place or service. The favorite illustration of the Lutheran doctrine is drawn from the history of the woman who touched the

---

[40] Latin for "the power of the Holy Spirit apart from the incidentals [of the Lord's Supper]."

hem of our Savior's garment. As there was always supernatural virtue in him, which flowed out to all who applied to him in faith, so there is in the sacraments. The Reformed doctrine is illustrated by a reference to our Savior's anointing the eyes of the blind man with the clay. There was no virtue in the clay to make the man see, the effect was due to the attending power of Christ. The modern rationalists smile at all these distinctions and say it all amounts to the same thing. These three views, however, are radically different in themselves, and have produced radically different effects, where they have severally prevailed.

All the points, both negative and positive, included in the statement of the Reformed doctrine, above given, are clearly presented with perfect unanimity in their symbolical books. In the Gallic Confession, Article 34, it is said, "We acknowledge, that these external signs are such, that through them God operates by the power of his Holy Spirit." The Helvetic Confession, ii. c. 19, says, "We do not sanction the doctrine that grace and the things signified are so bound to the signs or included in them, that those who" receive the signs receive also the blessings they represent. When this fails, the fault is indeed in the receiver; just as in the case of the Word, God in both offers his grace. His Word does not cease to be true and divine, nor do the sacraments lose their integrity, because men do not receive them in faith and to their salvation. See chapter 21, at the end. The Consensus Tigurinus teaches, as we have already seen, that the sacraments have no virtue in themselves, as means of grace: "If any good is conferred upon us by the sacraments, it is not owing to any proper virtue in them... For it is God alone who acts by his Spirit.[41] In the following articles it is taught that they benefit only believers, that grace is not tied to

---

[41] Hodge quotes the Latin here from Article 12 of the Consensus Tigurinus: "Si quid boni nobis per sacramenta confertur, id non Jit propria eorum virtute... Deus enim solus est , qui Spiritu suo agit."

them, that believers receive elsewhere the same grace, and that the blessing often follows long after the administration. The Scotch Confession, chapter 21, teaches that the whole benefit flows "from faith apprehending Christ, who alone renders the sacraments efficacious." In the Geneva Catechism, the question is asked: "Do you believe that the power and efficacy of the sacrament, instead of being included in the element, flow entirely from the Spirit of God? Answer: So I believe, that is, should it please the Lord to exercise his power through his own instruments to the end to which he has appointed them." It is not worthwhile to multiply quotations, for as to this point, there was no diversity of opinion. We would only refer the reader to Calvin's *Institutes*, iv. 14, a passage, which though directed against the Romanists, has a much wider scope. He there declares it to be a purely diabolical error to teach men to expect justification from the sacraments, instead of from faith; and insists principally on two things: first, that nothing is conferred through the sacraments beyond what is offered in the word; and, secondly, that they are not necessary to salvation, the blessings may be had without them. He confirms his own doctrine by the saying of Augustine: "It is possible for there to be invisible sanctification without a visible sign, and again, a visible sign without true sanctification."[42]

Such then, as we understand it, is the true doctrine of the Reformed church on the Lord's Supper. By the Reformed church, we mean the Protestant churches of Switzerland, the Palatinate, France, Belgium, England, Scotland and elsewhere. According to the public standards of these churches: The Lord's Supper is a holy ordinance instituted by Christ, as a memorial of his death, wherein, under the symbols of bread and wine, his body as broken for us and his blood as shed for the remission of sins, are signified,

---

[42] Hodge quotes the Latin here: "Invisibilem sanctificationem sine visibili signo esse posse, et visibile rursum signum sine vera sanctificatione."

Reformed Protestant Doctrine of the Lord's Supper

and, by the power of the Holy Ghost, sealed and applied to believers; whereby their union with Christ and their mutual fellowship are set forth and confirmed, their faith strengthened, and their souls nourished unto eternal life.

Christ is really present to his people, in this ordinance, not bodily, but by his Spirit; not in the sense of local nearness, but of efficacious operation. They receive him, not with the mouth, but by faith; they receive his flesh, not as flesh, not as material particles, nor its human life, but his body as broken and his blood as shed. The union thus signified and effected, between him and them is not a corporeal union, nor a mixture of substances, but spiritual and mystical, arising from the indwelling of the Spirit. The efficacy of this sacrament, as a means of grace, is not in the signs, nor in the service, nor in the minister, nor in the word, but solely in the attending influence of the Holy Ghost. This we believe to be a fair statement of the doctrine of the
Reformed church.

Other books by Gary Steward

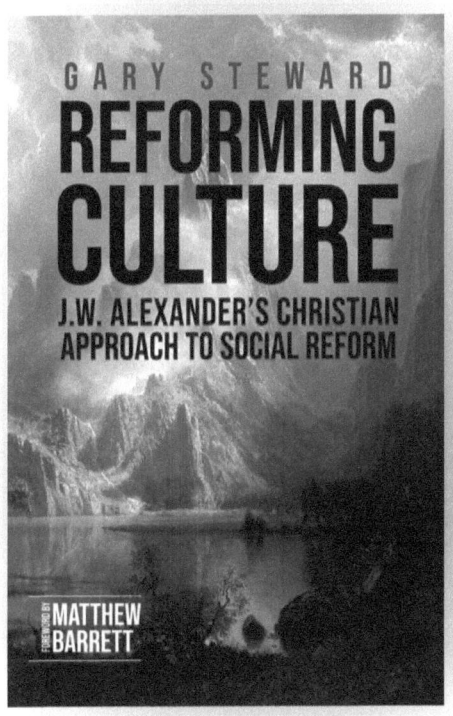

Scripture Index

Old Testament

Numbers
   3:32 145
Deuteronomy
   10:6 145
1 Samuel
   2:35 145
1 Kings
   2:35 145
   19:10 142
   19:18 .... 136, 142

2 Chronicles
   33:4-5 144
Psalms
   72 156
   133 149
Isaiah
   53 156
   61 135
Jeremiah
   7:4 91

New Testament

Matthew
   7:20 15
   12:24 80
   16:18 136
   16:19 95
   23:27 92
   28:20 137
Luke
   20:47 92
John
   6:33 205
   6:45 85
   6:54 203
   6:54-58 203

   10 63
   10:28 87
   18:36 88
Acts
   1:11 205
   8:37 123
   13:48 52
   19:39 47
   20:21 50

Romans
   1:5 50
   1:6 51
   8:9 60

8:16 63
8:17 63
8:23 52
8:28 51
8:30 52
9:24 53
9:29 54
11:2 146
14:17 88

1 Corinthians
1:2 .... 51, 52
1:9 53
1:18 52
1:24 51
1:26 54
6:15 167
6:19 .... 62, 167
12:13 60
7: 53

2 Corinthians
1:20 138
2:15 52

Galatians
1:15 53
5:8 53
5:13 53

Ephesians
1:11 52
1:18 54
1:22 60
3:10 48
4:4 53
4:4–6 73

4:15 60
4:16 60
5:23 177
5:25-26 48
5:25–27 89
5:25–30 63
5:30 203

Philippians
3:14 54

Colossians
1:18 60
3:15 53

1 Thessalonians
2:12 53
2:24 53
4:17 138

2 Thessalonians
2 157
2:11 52

1 Timothy
4:1 143
6:12 53

2 Timothy
1:9 53
3:4 143

Hebrews
2:11-14 166
3:1 54
9:5 53
10:10 52

1 Peter
1:2 52
2:4 62

2:5 62	2:19–20 .... 111, 112
2:9 54	2:20 86
2 Peter	2:27 86
1:10 54	4:1 23
2 Peter	Jude
2:1 143	1:18 143
3:3 143	Revelation
	2:9 24
	3:9 24
1 John	17:14 51
2:27 72	